Will Work from Home

Earn the Cash—
Without the Commute

Tory Johnson and
Robyn Freedman Spizman

BERKLEY BOOKS, NEW YORK

THE BERKLEY PUBLISHING GROUP
Published by the Penguin Group
Penguin Group (USA) Inc.
375 Hudson Street, New York, New York 10014, USA
Penguin Group (Canada), 90 Eglinton Avenue East, Suite 700, Toronto, Ontario M4P 2Y3, Canada (a division of Pearson Penguin Canada Inc.)
Penguin Books Ltd., 80 Strand, London WC2R 0RL, England
Penguin Group Ireland, 25 St. Stephen's Green, Dublin 2, Ireland (a division of Penguin Books Ltd.)
Penguin Group (Australia), 250 Camberwell Road, Camberwell, Victoria 3124, Australia (a division of Pearson Australia Group Pty. Ltd.)
Penguin Books India Pvt. Ltd., 11 Community Centre, Panchsheel Park, New Delhi—110 017, India
Penguin Group (NZ), 67 Apollo Drive, Rosedale, North Shore, 0632, New Zealand (a division of Pearson New Zealand Ltd.)
Penguin Books (South Africa) (Pty.) Ltd., 24 Sturdee Avenue, Rosebank, Johannesburg 2196, South Africa

Penguin Books Ltd., Registered Offices: 80 Strand, London WC2R 0RL, England

This publication is designed to provide accurate and authoritative information in regard to the subject matter covered. It is sold with the understanding that the publisher is not engaged in rendering legal, accounting, or other professional services. If you require legal advice or other expert assistance, you should seek the services of a competent professional. Nothing in this book is intended as an express or implied warranty of the suitability or fitness of any product, service, or design. The reader wishing to use a product, service, or design discussed in this book should first consult a specialist or professional to ensure suitability and fitness for the reader's particular lifestyle and environmental needs.

While the authors have made every effort to provide accurate telephone numbers and Internet addresses at the time of publication, neither the publisher nor the authors assume any responsibility for errors, or for changes that occur after publication. Further, publisher does not have any control over and does not assume any responsibility for author or third-party websites or their content.

PRINTING HISTORY
Berkley trade paperback edition: August 2008

Library of Congress Cataloging-in-Publication Data

Johnson, Tory.
    Will work from home : earn the cash—without the commute / Tory Johnson, Robyn Freedman Spizman.—Berkley trade paperback ed.
        p. cm.
    Includes bibliographical references and index.
    ISBN 978-0-425-22285-0
  1. Home labor.   2. Telecommuting.   3. Home-based businesses.   I. Spizman, Robyn Freedman.
II. Title.
    HD2333.J65 2008
    331.25'67—dc22

                                                                          2008002389

PRINTED IN THE UNITED STATES OF AMERICA

10 9 8 7 6 5 4 3 2 1

acknowledgments

■ ■ ■

We wish to extend our sincerest thanks to the women who shared their knowledge and experience for this book. To Meredith Bernstein, who supported our vision of a book on working from home. To our outstanding editor, Adrienne Avila at Berkley Publishers and the Penguin Group, who championed our efforts and secured a yes. We thank you for your bright ideas and clear vision. To the talented team at Berkley, including publisher Leslie Gelbman, managing editor Pam Barricklow, copyeditor Jacky Sach, and designers Steven Ferlauto and Edwin Tse.

Our appreciation also goes to our work-at-home heroes, researchers and writers Evelyn Sacks, Laura Raines, and Rachel Chase. We are grateful to you all for your passion and professionalism on this project. To Willy Spizman and Jenny Corsey of the Spizman Agency for your ongoing promotional support. And a huge thanks to our families and friends who support our work, day in and day out. You make it all worthwhile.

And a special thanks from Tory Johnson to everyone at *Good Morning America* for giving me the gift of an enormous platform to educate an audience on the range of opportunities to work from home. The feedback and success of those *GMA* viewers fuel my commitment to this beat.

contents

■ ■ ■

Contents

Contents

• • ■

Introduction

On days when the boss is unbearable, the meetings are endless, commuter traffic is at a standstill, and your babysitter wants to leave early, you can't help but long for a change. There has to be a better way to manage your work and your life. Your job may fund life's necessities, but the soul-numbing grind leaves little time or energy for family, friends, and the pursuit of personal happiness.

Home is where your heart is, and it's often where you want to be, too. It's not that you're ready to retire from work. You'd just like a day that didn't require so much rushing, all of that driving, and so many distractions.

If you've ever wondered if you could work from home—whether you could earn real money from a job that satisfies and excites you, design your own office, and work in comfortable clothes on your own schedule—you are not alone. You've picked a great time to wonder.

A not-so-quiet revolution is underway in the American workplace. Inspired, or perhaps driven, by today's killer commutes, and the need to juggle multiple personal responsibilities, many wage earners are seeking a better alternative to spending the bulk of their waking hours in a car and a cube. People are leaving the office, ditching the traffic, and heading home to work in record numbers. The phenomenon is called teleworking, and it is working: More employers are embracing the idea and more individuals are benefiting from it.

Thanks to advances in technology, a global economy, and corporate America's drive to more efficiently turn a profit, a growing number of people are performing their jobs remotely from outside the traditional office. Others are taking advantage of new trends like flextime and job sharing. They're switching to more enlightened employers or leaving to start their own businesses.

What everyone is looking for is greater satisfaction in work and more control over their personal lives. We know, because you told us, in no uncertain terms.

A Word from Tory Johnson

It started in 2006, when, as Workplace Contributor for ABC's *Good Morning America*, I reported on the American worker's desire for flexibility on the job and the opportunity to make money from home. The response was immediate and overwhelming.

When I received thousands of e-mails on the subject, it was clear that a nerve was hit.

That incredible response led me to research and report on practical ways to find work outside the office and to offer suggestions for how people could achieve better work/life balance. The research took me well beyond my role as "TV Expert," to become an active career coach and advocate for viewers. It was a comfortable role, since that's part of what I do in my job as CEO of Women For Hire, the first and only company to produce recruiting events and services for professional women to connect with top employers. As *Good Morning America*'s go-to gal on the subject, I answered and advised countless viewers who called, sent e-mails, or wrote letters with specific questions and challenging situations.

Viewers wrote to ask: How can I break away from the cube and ditch the commute? How can I control my hours to care for my elderly parents? How can I make money without paying exorbitant child-care costs? Are there ways to bring in extra cash to pay for vacation and holiday celebrations? What can I do to earn a living if physical or emotional challenges prevent outside work? How can I increase my income in retirement? Is it possible to be a stay-at-home mom and still have a career? How can I be sure a work-from-home opportunity is a legitimate business and not a scam?

It was as if women and men from all over the country, in different circumstances and for diverse reasons, were holding signs with variations of the same message—Will Work from Home.

As I traveled and spoke at my Women For Hire career expos, the topic of how to work from home came up repeatedly. I was stopped in airports and on the street by people seeking a nugget of advice. I realized that everyone needed more than quick answers and suggestions. They wanted a trusted guide.

A Word from
Robyn Freedman Spizman

For me, it started when I retired from teaching art and became a stay-at-home mom. I immediately began working at home. A fellow educator suggested I write a book, and while I had no clue how to do it, I figured it out, secured an agent, and got published.

It wasn't easy, but it taught me that income opportunities were still available to me, in or out of the traditional workplace, and that I was capable of learning to do anything (well, almost anything!). At that time, there weren't as many work-at-home choices available, so I created my own. An entrepreneur at heart, I taught art classes at home and started a public relations firm to book clients for media appearances.

Wanting to further my own business, I decided to promote myself. I called the local NBC station WXIA-TV and told producers about my first book. That got me a spot on a talk show, where I became a regular, appearing weekly. Twenty-six years later, I'm still featured on the local station plus national television, including appearances reporting on gift-giving for NBC's *Today* show. I am also heard on Star 94 (Star94.com) with *The Giftionary Show*, based on my book, with the talented radio hosts and afternoon drive team of Cindy and Ray.

One of my regular segments became a hallmark of my success. Every time I did a segment called "Money for Moms," the phones would light up at the station and we'd be bombarded with calls and requests for information. I began speaking often on ways that women could make money from home. Along the way, I met hundreds of women who had been successful and I had the great pleasure of featuring their products and services on television.

Like me, these women were working from home, figuring out how to make money and find fulfillment. Even in 1981, it was clear that women were struggling with their different roles and how to make them work together.

It was inevitable that Tory and I would team up to write books to empower women. We both believe that when women put their minds to it, they can accomplish what they set out to do. We also know the power of shared know-how and encouragement. If others can do it, so can you.

How to Get the Most from This Book

Now, more than ever, "Will Work from Home" is a sign of our times. It's a sign that says American workers are worn out and stressed by the traditional ways of work.

They're fed up with having little say in how they spend their time and needing to sacrifice financial stability for personal endeavors, or vice versa. But this sign also tells us that these workers are resourceful, hopeful, and willing to learn new ways of supporting themselves and their dreams.

We have never seen a topic resonate so deeply with so many.

As we travel and work around the country, women constantly ask us about the possibilities of working from home. Do the opportunities really exist? How can I find them? How do I know which one is right for me? We wrote this guide in response to all those questions, and the unspoken longings they represent. Maybe your need is to spend more time with your children, stretch a one-paycheck budget to include some fun, put your urban skills to work in the resort where you want to retire, or launch that small business that keeps coming to mind.

It excites us to see people taking the initiative to change their lives because we know there are real solutions. We've looked for and found many. We've called on our own career expertise and the insider knowledge of seasoned working-from-home veterans to create the kind of guide you can use now to start moving toward more meaningful and profitable work.

In this book you'll find four clear-cut paths that will lead you to making money at home. You can take your current position home, fill an existing need with a company that will hire you from home, start a business on a small budget, or follow your passion into direct sales. You'll be able to explore the variations, advantages, and disadvantages of each.

You may already have your heart set on one particular path. For example, you have a job you like, but you'd really love it if you could do it from home several days a week. In that case, you can go straight to the section on talking to your boss about a flexible work accommodation. If, however, you're not sure which direction you want to take—except to know that you need a change—then you'll want to go through each chapter to learn more about your options.

If you're willing to work from home, and change the way you live and work, we invite you to put down the sign and stick with this guide. You have a journey ahead, but as you'll see, others have already blazed the trail. Many workers have followed these proven paths home. We believe you can, too. We're rooting for your success every step of the way.

Go make it happen!

—Tory Johnson and Robyn Freedman Spizman

chapter one

Home Is Where the Job Is

In a perfect world, we'd all sleep late, stay in our pajamas on days when we're worn out, and have the time to do exactly what we want. We'd never punch a time clock, attend another meeting, or pick up fast food on the way home from a Little League game. We'd have prepared a fresh salad, pasta sauce, and cupcakes in advance, because we'd have the time. But real life isn't always conducive to such. Instead, we're late to the meeting, we're probably going to miss the first four innings of the game, and afterward, it'll be burgers or pizza. Why can't we turn that luxury-of-time fantasy into a reality?

Um . . . wait, we can. Suddenly, the choices we have to work from home, to set our own schedule, to be our own boss, and call the shots are exploding. To borrow from science, what we're seeing is the equivalent of a "Big Bang," and we're dealing with an enormous money-making opportunity. There's a whole new business universe out there, and it's changing the way many women and men work and live.

The myth is that homemakers eat bonbons, watch soaps, and take care of their kids. The reality is that there's a new revolution of people staying home these days and they're doing a whole lot more than folding laundry; they are moms and dads, new grads and grandparents, skilled professionals, and high-powered executives.

These individuals are finding more energy, more time, more ways to make money, and yes, they're doing it their way. So, if working from home is where your heart is, you are in the right place. It's definitely the right time.

What's This "Big Bang" of Opportunity?

According to the astronomers, the world as we know it, with all its galaxies, stars, and planets, started with a giant explosion. That set everything in motion and changed the universe. We don't know for sure that this is the way it happened, but we do know that the earth is here and that it works because of certain forces like gravity and circling the sun.

Okay, the "Big Bang" may be a slight exaggeration, but what we're seeing in society and the business world is a less galactic, but no less powerful, explosion of new ideas and attitudes caused by some dramatic trends that have been percolating underneath the surface for a decade or more.

These forces, or trends, are changing the way we think about work and its effect on our lives. They're making it easier for all of us to work from home, or the park, or the local coffee shop. Alternative working styles are no longer seen as a cop-out or a dropout from the traditional economy. They are very much a part of it—the smart, savvy part for people who want work to support their lives, not the other way around.

"Is it really possible? Can I really stay at home and make money?" We've heard that question asked by thousands of women and men across the country. Our resounding answer is "Yes!" This is the perfect time, because the world of work is growing and changing. It's less rigid and more fluid, less restrictive and more inclusive, less traditional and more innovative. Why?

It's partly the trends, which we'll explore a bit further. You're probably already aware of some of them. Others may be news to you. Together, they're creating that "Big Bang" of opportunity we mentioned—a new world with a galaxy of different job titles, small businesses, and ways to make money from home. These trends—and your own gumption—can take you out of the office, out of debt, out of your boring routine, and into a richer, fuller life.

Trends You Can Use to Change the World Right from Your Home

- Continuing advances in technology

- A global, changing workplace

- Emphasis on work/life balance

- A desire for more control

No matter what your needs, your skills, or your plans, these are trends to use. Let them encourage you. You're not the only one wondering if there isn't a better way to fit work into your life.

Others share your dreams. There's a whole army of smart, determined people out there who are overcoming the obstacles and finding solutions. You'll meet them as you journey through this guide.

There's a growing movement, a revolution going on, right now. It's real and wide and welcoming.

Tapping into the Trends

Whether you grew up with a laptop, or can remember rotary phones, computers have rocked your world. We live in an information age and a global economy because of technology. Think high-speed connections, the World Wide Web, PCs, cell phones, and Instant Imaging. We can connect and do business with people all over the world, from almost anywhere, including home.

In the '80s, students began taking courses through "distance learning." Now American surgeons train doctors in Third World countries using remote-controlled, computer-guided robots. You can learn how to design websites, a job that didn't exist in the '70s, as well as any other number of skills.

In the '90s, companies harnessed the power of e-commerce. Want to buy a computer, new towels, a car seat, or a vacation? Shop online. Now workers travel and meet online as well. No need to waste time and money traveling to a meeting when they can share thoughts, images, voice, and text, in real time, by teleconferencing.

Millions of Americans research a medical diagnosis, apply for college, search for a job, plan a vacation, buy clothing, or find their dream house online. No doubt, you're one of them.

Maybe you logged onto the Internet at school or the office, but it's just as likely that you have searched, or shopped, from your den or bedroom. Ah, and there's the difference. Technology isn't new. It's been around since before the Industrial Revolution. It's just that now it has advanced to bring the machine home to us. More afford-able and powerful computers and the spread of broadband have removed any technical barriers from working at home. We can change the world from our kitchens. We're all geeks, wired and ready to work right here, right now. Thank goodness for technology.

'Net Explosion of Jobs

Not only has the Internet revolutionized the way we work and live, but it has created an alternative job market with new companies, new job descriptions, and new opportunities. Think chefs only work in restaurants? Meet Jennifer Beisser, CEO of ChefsLine, a business that supplies "on demand culinary advice for busy cooks." Clients find the service online, but they use the phone line to con-nect with a chef who will share personalized advice, step-by-step cooking instructions, and those little touches that can turn an ordi-nary dinner into fine cuisine. That chef who's providing the advice is doing so from his or her own home.

"It's for people staring at the same old chicken breast and think-ing, 'Oh please, not again,'" says Beisser. "If they don't have time to read a cookbook, they can call our service, which is like having a cookbook that talks to you and works with you." ChefsLine.com is at the crossroads of connecting at-home cooks who want instant advice—and are willing to pay for it—with experts willing to dis-pense that advice from the home—and get paid to do so.

Are You Ready to Rocket?

Want to explore today's work-from-home job market? It's fast, easy, and so much bigger than you can imagine. Just let your fingers do the walking . . . across your keyboard. There's no limit to your reach. The world is your oyster. You could become an Internet researcher for people without computer skills, the local beat reporter for a publication in another city, or take orders for flowers or clothing by phone. You could offer financial advice online, solve technical or tax problems, or sell anything from travel packages to baby clothes. Your boss might live across the country or even the world. No worries, mate. You're connected.

It's Not Our Fathers' Business World

Big companies used to hire workers for the long haul. If you were loyal and productive, they'd promote you through the ranks and retire you with a gold watch and a pension. Now they're busy

---

The Movement in Numbers

- More than 70 percent of Americans are Internet users and more than half of them have high-speed connections. Those numbers are growing and so are home workers.
- Roughly 20 percent of the American workforce engages in telework at least one day per month. According to polls, the number of employers who allowed it grew by 63 percent to 12.4 million in 2006.
- Several studies estimate that 100 million U.S. workers will telework, at least part-time, by 2010—from 14.7 million teleworking in 2006 to 100 million—that's an explosion!
- Baby boomers are retiring in droves. The Telework Association and Council predicts an eight million shortfall of workers in the American market by 2014. Can you smell opportunity? You could fill the gap—from home.
- The entrepreneurial spirit is alive and well. The number of small business start-ups is growing. Small businesses are generating 60 to 80 percent of the new jobs in this country. That's big business and a big invitation to launch your own.

competing in a global economy and you're on your own. No more cradle to grave. Companies have slimmed down, automated, and closed factories. They've laid off workers, axed whole departments that didn't fit their needs, and shipped jobs overseas to cut costs.

If you've been in the workplace awhile, you've seen the upheaval, maybe even the pink slips. You know that a job or a company can change on a dime. If you're a new grad, you've heard the drill—you'll change jobs or careers up to seven or eight times in your working life.

There's been a lot of change, unrest, and even heartbreak in this job market. You've read about or been affected by the headlines—the bankruptcies, mergers, massive layoffs, bubbles, busts, scandals, and fraud. But there's positive news, too. Many American companies are leaner, smarter, and stronger, and so are American workers. We've learned to adapt, take on new skills, and negotiate for what we want. No more expectations for a lavish retirement send-off. We're taking responsibility for our own careers.

"Women are at the leading edge of shifting the career paradigm for everyone. They're no longer acting as agents of their employers, but as career 'self-agents,' using flexible work arrangements and setting their own terms of employment as a way to make work 'work,'" says professor Mary Shapiro, at the Simmons School of Management in Boston. Hooray for us!

We're deciding when, where, and how much we want to work, depending on our economic needs and life stage. After a baby, a death, or a family crisis, women often cut back or rearrange their work schedules. There are circumstances when time, attention, and caring are more important than money. Only about 18 percent of us stop work altogether, however, according to a Simmons/HP study. That's a significant figure. It tells us that more women are figuring out alternative ways to combine work and personal life, so they can do both. An obvious alternative is to work from home.

We All Need Balance

When women first entered the workforce in great numbers, we tried to do it the guys' way. The commute, the nine to five, the navy suits, and the Day-Timer. Some of us made it to the corner office and beyond. A lot of us found great satisfaction in our jobs, but we also learned that the guys' way only worked for guys. Most of them had wives at home taking care of the house and kids.

Are you tired of trying to do two jobs in different places in the same twenty-four hours, and feeling like you're failing at both? Are you exhausted, frustrated, burned out, and stressed? We're not talking about the kind of stress that a hot bath and candles is going to cure. We're talking about the effects of living too long with all work and no play—the screaming, stomach-knotting, hair-pulling kind of stress that spikes our risk for heart attack and stroke. Stress kills. Medical researchers keep doing new studies to prove that point and we know it in our gut.

So what's the answer? We don't want to quit work. We like it and we're good at it. What we want is time to go for a walk, read a book, spend time with our spouse, eat lunch with a friend, and watch our kid play baseball. While we're at it, we want to see the whole game . . . and the fourth-grade play . . . the school awards ceremony . . . our best friend's wedding rehearsal . . . and our parents' anniversary dinner. We want to be there for our lives—not just work through them—and we deserve to be. That isn't going to happen if we're chained to our desks, out of town, stuck in traffic, or working late through the events that matter.

What we want and need is some kind of balance—a balance of

work and life. Maybe it's our influence on the workplace, or maybe it's a changing society, but men have taken a hard look at the rat race, too. They've seen that in working long hours, traveling, transferring, and fighting their way up the ladder, they've missed a lot of ball games, too. Not to mention family dinners, vacations, and friendships. Is it worth it?

No. What good is a big salary if you never have time to enjoy it?

Companies Are Listening

Changing attitudes are causing dramatic shifts in the traditional workplace according to the Families and Work Institute. The old command-and-control style of authority, which worked when companies nurtured and groomed employees for their entire careers, no longer flies. Smart employers are figuring out that when employees are valued as people with real lives, not just time-clock punchers, they are happier and more productive.

Work environments are becoming more supportive. Ideas like flexible working hours, job sharing, onsite child-care centers, company gyms, and personal days off are commonplace in many companies now. These kinds of benefits are making it easier and more enjoyable for workers. They also make good sense for employers. Replacing an employee is expensive. Between the downtime when the job is unfilled and the costs of recruiting, hiring, and training a replacement, the price of replacing someone runs up to a third of an employee's annual salary, according to a study by the Society for Human Resource Management. It's cheaper to grant a few reasonable requests. So if you're a solid performer who wants to work from home, now's the time to ask. More bosses are listening.

They'll be listening even harder soon. There's an impending shortage of workers as baby boomers start retiring, and the younger generations don't have the numbers to fill all the jobs. They need you. That's the best time to negotiate. You've got leverage.

Companies are already discussing ways to keep the brain power of baby boomers on the payroll either by rehiring them as consultants where they set their own schedules, or letting them work part-time. The bottom line is that the American workforce is going to need everybody. Whether you want to find a job, change your job, go part-time, work from home, or combine work with college or retirement, your chances of finding a position you can work on your terms have never been better.

Teleworking Works

Teleworking—people working remotely from the office at home—is an idea whose time has come. Sure, bosses were skeptical at first. "If I send them home, how will I know they aren't napping or at the

Happy at Home

We can all learn from nurses. For years, nurses worked long hours at low salaries. Now there's a national shortage. The Department of Labor predicts that we will need one million more nurses by 2012. Guess what? As hospitals had to compete for a smaller pool of workers, these workers became more valuable.

Hospitals raised salaries and increased benefits such as signing bonuses, tuition reimbursement, and flexible scheduling. Many nurses work three 12-hour shifts a week and receive full-time health care and vacation benefits. That gives them four days a week to raise children, work a second job, explore a hobby, or take a class. Some nursing moms only work weekends or nights, so their spouses can care for the children and they don't have to spend on day care.

Hospitals are paying to retrain older nurses and bring them back into the workforce, and allow others to shorten their hours as they age.

mall?" It didn't happen. People appreciated the freedom and convenience. They liked the trust. Without interruptions they often worked better. Research backs that up. Studies show that teleworkers usually are more productive. They are happier and more engaged in their work.

Employees gain, but so do companies. Sending people home to work means less office space to buy or lease and fewer utilities to pay. That improves profits.

It's also better for the environment, according to the Clean Air Campaign. Carpooling, van-pooling and mass-transit all decrease traffic and pollution, but teleworking takes cars off the highway altogether.

Lawmakers enacted the Telework Enhancement Act of 2007, which says that all future government employees be eligible to telework, in part to decrease traffic in Washington. What they saw outside their government windows was gridlock.

The idea is just beginning to catch on, with the Patent and Trademark Office leading the way. It has nearly 700 patent examiners working from home at least four days a week. It plans to increase that to 3,000 teleworkers by 2011. According to the Telework Exchange, a public-private partnership focused on demonstrating the tangible value of telework, the average federal employee who works two days a week at home would reclaim 98 hours (now lost to commuting) and save $55.52 a month (with gas averaging $3 a gallon). Federal jobs can be found in all states—and the government is facing a worker shortage as well. Anyone care to apply and volunteer to work from home?

You don't have to know these trends to work from home, but doesn't it add to your confidence? There are going to be more people working from home in the future. There's no reason why you shouldn't be one of them.

One Solution for Many Needs

The beauty of this "Will Work from Home" movement is that one solution is the answer to so many different scenarios.

Not working isn't an option. We need to support or totally earn our household budgets. We just want a better way of doing it so that we can feel more successful at both. Wouldn't working at home simplify our lives, save us time and possibly money? Probably.

If you interrupted a career you love to stay home and raise your children, your issues are slightly different. You plan to continue your career someday, but you need a way to keep your contacts fresh and your skills sharp. You need a flexible job at home.

An at-home job is also a solution for fathers who want to get off the corporate treadmill, take more control of their careers, and play a greater role in parenting.

It's an answer for singles and couples without children who want more freedom to pursue hobbies, volunteer in the community, or travel. It's ideal for those with health challenges that preclude them from working outside the home.

If you're a baby boomer who is ready to lose the five-day week, nine-to-five schedule, but not ready to rock on the front porch, keep reading. A job at home or your own business could take you closer to your grandchildren or the golf course. It could offer work that is more fun or challenging and grow your retirement income.

Some of you may desperately need to take time off from the office routine to care for aging parents, or a spouse or child with a chronic illness. You may find yourself living in a different city or a remote area with massive unemployment or few jobs. If you have physical or medical limitations, you need real work that you can do without a commute. You may be newly widowed or divorced and need a way to support yourself.

Happy at Home

Chef Erika Connell Cooper knew that she wanted to work with food by age fourteen. She held jobs in bakeries, catering companies, and restaurants before entering the New England Culinary Institute. After a job as a baking consultant with King Arthur Flour, she earned a bachelor's degree in food and beverage management.

Teaching business courses at her culinary institute, she met her husband, a fellow chef. In one year, the couple married, had a daughter, Greta, and moved to upstate Vermont. "We both felt that one of us should stay home with Greta, and for lots of reasons the best choice seemed to be me," she says. "I can't begin to tell you the feeling of isolation—being in a remote area of New England in winter with a newborn baby—but we made it."

After eight months, her husband became the executive chef for a restaurant chain, and the couple moved back to Massachusetts near family. Cooper continued to stay home with her daughter, and did some catering and teaching. When she had a job, her husband or parents kept Greta.

"I was fortunate to know a group of women who had left careers in the hotel industry, retail, and teaching to raise their children. We were all trying to figure out together [how to work and stay home]," she says. "Being an at-home parent is so challenging in lots of ways. Until I went back to part-time teaching and had conversations outside my home about my passion for cooking, I didn't realize how much I'd missed that. I knew that I had to find a way to work that let me remain committed to my family."

Listening to Tory Johnson on *Good Morning America* from a new home in Wisconsin, Cooper found a perfect opportunity, in ChefsLine, a company that hires chefs to give on-demand cooking advice to clients.

"When I called, I found that they were looking for people with culinary and customer-service skills, so I began working on the Chefs Hotline and doing consulting about twenty hours a week. This job gave me the flexibility I needed to work and stay home with my daughter," says Cooper.

After meeting owner Jennifer Beisser at a conference, Cooper also became the national director for marketing and sales for the company, a job that lets her use her cooking and business skills at home. "I'm using my brain again and have a renewed sense of faith in myself," says Cooper.

As much as she cherished the time with her daughter, Cooper felt like a part of her life was missing. "This is exactly the kind of thing I wanted to be doing. It's giving us some breathing room financially, and I can take the job with me if we move again. I feel so fortunate to have found this balance. I count my blessings every day."

Is the office grind killing your creativity? You're stifled working at a desk during the day. Your creative juices start flowing at 2:00 in the morning, not 2:00 in the afternoon. You need larger blocks of time to write, design or plan, time that isn't interrupted by meetings, office politics or coworkers. Home is the working environment you need.

On the other hand, if you're a stay-at-home mom, interruptions by other adults may be exactly what you're missing. A part-time job at home could provide welcome mental stimulation, and ease the stresses of a one-budget household. Imagine dinners out, a luxury vacation, college savings, or more money to spend on gifts for the holidays.

If you're a student, we know you need cash. The trouble is that you already have a full schedule of classes and study, a schedule that fluctuates. What if you could earn money with your computer from your dorm room or at home in the summer? No more begging the fast-food boss to let you off for your family vacation or to volunteer at the hospital.

Cash, career, convenience, necessity. No matter what your situation, background or monetary goals, "Will Work from Home" can be your solution.

Proven Paths to Working from Home

We could list all the different jobs you could do or businesses you could start from home, but that wouldn't be a guide. It would be a doorstop!

Instead, we're going to show you four proven paths that can lead you home to work. You'll be able to adapt one of these paths to your own situation, especially as we're going to give you the advice, resources, inspirational stories, and checklists you'll need for the journey.

First Path: ASK THE BOSS

If you're working and satisfied with your job, but not its location, this could be your easiest path home. All you have to do is convince your boss that you can be just as effective, maybe even more so, working from your spare bedroom as your third-floor cubicle. Not good at asking? You'll find step-by-step directions in chapter three for writing and presenting a professional "Will Work from Home" proposal, what to say to overcome common objections, and strategies to make the transition easier.

Second Path: FILL A NEED

Many employers are looking for individuals who can work from home: people to answer calls, provide customer service, give technical assistance, or perform virtual office tasks, such as handling administrative tasks. There are also companies, law firms, government agencies, and nonprofit organizations willing to set workers up at home. You could be their next hire. We'll supply you with leads on how to find employers that are hiring today, and tell you how to find others.

Third Path: BE YOUR OWN BOSS

Obviously, if you're running the show, you get to say where you work, right? This could be the right time to launch a small business based on a professional skill or personal passion, hobby, craft, or service that you can provide. It doesn't have to be a huge venture requiring a large capital investment and a five-year plan. It might be something as simple as planning children's birthday parties for busy moms, or driving seniors to doctors' appointments. This chapter will have you thinking like an entrepreneur and acting like a business owner. We'll show you ways to start a business with a little cash and a lot of confidence.

Fourth Path: BECOME A DIRECT SALES PRO

Think beyond Avon, Mary Kay, and Tupperware. The number of companies selling their products and services outside of stores, in people's homes, or online has mushroomed tremendously. If you've got a passion for wine, spa treatments, or educational toys, just to name a few products, there's a company out there that wants to put your passion to work. Start-up costs are usually small, and you can set your own hours and schedule. You'll read profiles of many of these companies and advice from successful direct sales professionals. Direct sales can be a second job to fund a fantastic vacation or pay off debts. Or, it could be your breakthrough career—the one that gives your life meaning, satisfaction, and bucks for your bank account.

Each path has its pros and cons. So does working from home in general. It's a lifestyle for many, but not everyone. Before you take the plunge, here are some things to consider.

Working-from-Home Rewards

There are obvious advantages to working from home. Here's what people who are happy at home have to say:

- Having your job and life in the same place is more convenient and comfortable. Think sweat clothes and sneakers instead of heels and business suits.

- You have greater control over your schedule. No more coffee at ten o'clock in the break room, listening to whining coworkers. Mail a package, sit on the deck, do some yoga, take a bath whenever you want or need a break.

- No commute. Your workday can be shorter and more productive. A walk up the stairs or down the hall to your home office is certainly less stressful than thirty to forty-five minutes on the interstate. Instead of driving home, you could be exercising, calling friends, or helping the kids with their homework.

- Your career could improve. You might have more time and energy for professional associations and networking because of a shorter workday.

- You'll save money on gas, car maintenance, and parking fees, not to mention business clothes, lunches out, and gifts for coworkers.

- You may be able to work part-time, full-time, or during non-business hours. If there's no set time you have to be at your desk, you can work weekends or nights in order to reduce or eliminate the need for child care.

- You can participate more in your community as a volunteer or go to a doctor without clearing it with your boss. You can be home with a sick child, travel more with your spouse, and possibly relocate without changing jobs.

- A virtual job can widen your career prospects, particularly if you live in a remote area or in a high-unemployment market.

- It feels great when you have more control over your life or more cash in the bank. Saving time and money while gaining peace of mind can be a perfect working solution.

Some Precautions

- The arrangement is not for everyone. Working from home is still work. No one makes $1,000 a week stuffing envelopes— that's a scam. A job at home usually demands the same level of professionalism, focus, and determination as one at the office, sometimes even more.

- You'll need to convert some space in your home to an office, and equip it with the technology to communicate with the outside world. You'll also have to learn how to avoid home distractions during working hours and ignore business calls during family time.

- You may still need to pay for child care because professional work and toddlers don't mix.

- You could lose health-care insurance, vacation, and other benefits, as many jobs from home are for contract workers. This is not as big a drawback if your income is secondary to the household budget. It's a much larger consideration if you're the sole breadwinner.

- If you're a contractor, consultant, or small-business owner, you'll need to keep good financial records for tax purposes. The upside is you'll be able to write off business expenses.

- If you are an employee with benefits, being at home might slow down your career advancement. This doesn't have to be, but you'll need to know ways to remind your boss that you're working just as hard, or harder, than your coworkers in the office.

- Finally, it takes a certain kind of personality to work successfully from home. It helps to be a self-starter and problem solver.

Managing your time and work flow will be your responsibility. If you're an extrovert who thrives on relationships, or works best with input from team members, being at home by yourself isn't going to feel comfortable. It might even make you miserable.

One person's reward may be another's stumbling block. The quiet of home might be a haven to one and sheer boredom to another. Your chances of success improve when you know what's important to you and have realistic expectations. Every new job or life change has a learning curve and some trade-offs. Your job search will require some introspection and assessment, goal-setting, research, and effort, but you don't have to do it alone.

The Purpose of a Guide

We're going to be with you as you plan and pursue your journey. We'll tell you what to pack and what to expect. We've mapped the curves, charted the hills, seen the views, and marked the rough spots. We know where to find the rest stops and where to turn for help. It's your path and your life, but everyone needs encouragement. You'll find lots of it in the stories and advice from the seasoned hikers who have already made their way home to work.

Whether you choose a quick and easy path or a longer one, you'll be able to find useful directions and the practical resources you need here to help you make every step.

ACTION STEPS—*Home Is Where the Job Is*

1. *Buy a notebook and write down why you want or need to work from home.* What would be your ideal dream job? How many hours would you work and when? How much would you make? How would it make

you feel? How do you envision it improving your life? What would you do with the money? Be specific about describing your dreams. It will make your job search later more focused and personal. You'll be able to eliminate those options that don't fit what you want.

2. *Perform a candid personality assessment.* Will you be bored working alone? Will you be distracted by people, things, or chores in your home? Will you be motivated to get to your desk and stay focused until tasks are complete? Be honest with yourself.

3. *Connect with one new resource every day.* Commit to working on your goal daily by reaching out to one new resource, which could be a website, a group, or an individual. Call someone you know who works from home and ask about the highs and lows. Reach message boards in chat rooms of your favorite social networking websites to learn about how other people are making money at home. The idea is to seek new information every day. The daily commitment reinforces that you're truly determined to make this goal a reality.

■ ■ ■

chapter two

Homebound Readiness

Do you consider "work" a noun—a place where you go, put in your time, and come home? Or is it a verb—something you actively pursue? If you answered "verb," you've probably got the drive, motivation, and moxie to make it from home.

Before hanging out a shingle that announces you're in business, it's important to review the characteristics of a successful home worker. We'll help you to assess your skill set to see what you've already got and what you could use more of. And we'll help you see what it will take to make the transition from someone else's space to your own.

Many people who make the switch are pleasantly surprised to learn that skills perfected at work and those honed at home can blend so well in a home-based career or part-time job. You may already have more in your work-at-home toolbox than you realize.

We've prepared a short quiz you can use to assess your

entrepreneurial spirit and motivations. It's a nonthreatening (ungraded!) test of your commitment to going it from home.

"Hired at Home"—the Five-Minute Readiness Quiz

It's hard to resist self-assessment quizzes. Although they're fun, they rarely lead to a definitive answer and probably shouldn't be used that way. The value is in helping you visualize what you need to do to get from where you are to where you think you want to be.

That's the spirit in which we've designed this quiz. Invest about five minutes and learn some valuable facts about yourself. Are you ripe and ready to bear the fruits of at-home labor? Or do you have some growing yet to do? Let's find out.

1. **Have you been considering the idea of working from home for six months or longer?**

   yes _____

   no _____

   not really _____

2. **If you've told anyone else about your idea, has the response been positive, as in, "Wow, that sounds perfect for you?!"**

   yes _____

   no _____

   not really _____

3. **Have you sought out anyone who works successfully from home and asked questions about how it really works?**

   yes _____

   no _____

   not really _____

4. Do people (including yourself) consider you a disciplined
   self-starter who enjoys working independently without
   constant feedback?

   yes _____

   no _____

   not really _____

5. Once you get an idea in your head, do you typically pursue it until
   you've achieved it? Are you persistent?

   yes _____

   no _____

   not really _____

6. Do you consider your workplace your primary source of friends
   and social connections?

   yes _____

   no _____

   not really _____

7. Do you constantly crave the company of others? For example, do
   you feel lonely after a few hours at home alone on a weekend?

   yes _____

   no _____

   not really _____

8. Do you have strong powers of concentration and an ability to
   ignore distractions?

   yes _____

   no _____

   not really _____

9. Do you consider yourself a highly organized person who knows how to manage time and tasks?

yes _____

no _____

not really _____

10. Do you typically set goals, make lists, and in other ways measure your progress?

yes _____

no _____

not really _____

Let's Review!

As promised, no grades. But let's review and interpret your answers together. Hopefully you've answered "no" on questions 6 and 7 and "yes" on the others. If not, don't fret! Remember that the quiz is not a black-and-white predictor of future success. It's a tool to help you better understand where you are in your decision-making process.

Take a look first at Questions 6 and 7, the ones about your work style. We all work for different reasons, and social connection is a common one. But if work is your primary playground and you have few friends outside the office, retreating to a back bedroom converted into an office may not be right for you. It's important to consider your lifestyle and the way you interact and socialize.

For many busy people, especially parents of young children, work is basically their only adult social time. Giving that up can leave some people grumpy and unsatisfied.

We know a couple who have both worked for more than thirty years, he in a downtown office and she at home. Five days a week, he schedules a lunch date with a client or friend and enjoys that hour and a half in a restaurant immeasurably. She cheerfully microwaves the previous night's leftovers, rarely sees anyone but the mailman, and loves the more solitary, but satisfying, rhythm of her days. Their individual styles closely reflect their personalities. We think they've both chosen wisely and so do they.

Question 8 is an especially important one. Although you can learn or adapt skills you might be lacking (for example, your ability to concentrate can be enhanced with practice, the use of ear plugs, or a good babysitter), some factors are more inherent in your personality and harder to change.

Let's look at the other questions, to which you've ideally answered yes.

Question 1. Having reflected on the possibility of working at home for a while without talking yourself out of it is a good indication that you should continue to pursue the idea. We know you didn't pick this book up the very first day you considered going inside. That tells us you're getting pretty serious about it and that you're willing to invest in the process.

Question 2. The reactions of people who know you can be a reasonably good indication of whether the idea makes sense for you. Of course the ultimate choice should be yours, but solid input can help expand your perspective.

If your best friend erupts with a loud, "What *are* you thinking?!" when you share your ideas with her, don't get upset. Ask why she reacted so strongly and challenge her to produce some solid thoughts about why she thinks this might or might not work for you.

Question 3. Conducting research is a sign that you're getting serious. Research can be informal, such as asking questions of someone you know or reading a few websites. Or it can be more formally pursued by assigning yourself a list of relevant books or sitting down with a career counselor. The important thing is to begin to gather information and not be afraid of what you learn.

Question 4. The ability to work independently with minimal response from others is a big factor in your potential success as an at-home worker. Those who have hired you, or those who buy your product or service, want to know they're doing business with someone who will take the ball and run with it, regardless of location. Even if you're still on someone else's payroll, working at home makes you much more your own boss than ever before.

Question 5. Stick-to-itiveness is essential for successful employment in general, and especially for those who work independently. It means you're likely to actually make this work-at-home thing happen. It also suggests that once you're up and running, you're likely to meet deadlines and commitments. (Experienced freelancers tell us that getting the work in and on time is the primary reason they're rehired by clients.)

Question 8. Beware—offices are filled with plenty of potential diversions, but nowhere near as many as home. They're everywhere. The arrival of a dress you ordered online, the ringing of the home phone (and your desire to see if it's your best friend calling about weekend plans), the sound of the kids in the family room, the crusty breakfast dishes in the sink, last week's ironing, the garden that must be watered . . . You get the idea.

All compete for your attention, but when home is your workplace you need the steely discipline to ignore all these and more during your dedicated work hours.

Questions 9 and 10. Organization is the mother's milk of the home-working woman. Or something like that. The more orderly and efficient you are, the more you can concentrate on *any* type of work. It's even more true at home where you may be setting your own work hours while juggling family duties. Organization can take diverse forms, many of which we touch on in later chapters—from an orderly work space to a well-run home that doesn't demand your attention when you should be on the job, from a clear mind to a computer that's not shared by other family members.

If you're a list maker, you're probably someone who likes to set and meet goals. This is so important when you're establishing your own benchmarks rather than receiving marching orders from someone else. Similarly, working independently means you have to monitor your own progress. If the bus drops the kids off at three and you're headed to baseball practice and the orthodontist, you've got to be certain you'll be able to meet that day's goals despite the distractions.

Get Tough!

If self-starting, goal setting, and persistence don't define you at the moment, you'll need to take a hard look at your situation. There are two choices—get the essential skills you lack, or reconsider your goals. Whether you develop a home-based enterprise or convince your current boss to cut you loose, you're going to need to be strong, even tough.

Working at home can be distracting, fattening, lonely, even isolating for some people, especially for team players who take most of their strength and motivation from others.

Your clients, your boss, and your coworkers want to know that just because you're not around doesn't mean you're not as inspired, efficient, and productive as everybody else. (In fact some people who work from home say they have to be even more productive, especially at the beginning, to justify their homebound status.)

Discover Your Path

On her entertaining and inspiring website, EscapeFromCubicle
Nation.com, writer Pamela Slim offers "Five Easy Ways to Discover
What You Are Meant to Do with Your Life." The exercise suggests
that a career path can sometimes present itself through our creative
preferences.

Answer the following questions and look for clues about the
real you:

1. *What is your favorite movie?* Is it action-packed, intellectual,
   foreign, or perhaps romantic? What do the characters say and
   do that moves or excites you?

2. *What are your favorite TV channels or programs?* Do you love
   to learn or do you watch tube to escape? Do you seek out
   reality-based shows, programs about business, or specials
   on the arts?

3. *What kinds of museums do you like?* Are you a nut for modern
   photography or do you prefer natural history? Do you feel
   more connected to the ancient past than the future? Do you
   like passive viewing or active participation?

4. *What music do you prefer?* What singers, styles, and lyrics touch
   your soul?

5. *What kinds of outdoor spaces do you most enjoy?* Do mountains
   make your heart sing or do you dream of living by the ocean?
   Do you love to be active and even take risks in nature, or would
   you rather admire it from a distance?

The exercise doesn't take long (we tried it) and it just may help you begin to see patterns about your life. Your personal interests may influence your professional goals.

Mine Your Motivations

When you think about working from home, do you picture yourself sitting at your kitchen table in comfy clothes with a steaming cup of tea at hand? Able to throw in a load of laundry on a whim while getting "loads" of work done because you have no commute and few meetings?

Sounds good, but beyond that romantic vision of your new, at-home-working self, what really are your motivations? What's in it for you? Does what you *want* to achieve match what you *can* achieve? Let's look at motivations.

The reasons people work from home are as diverse as the people themselves. Among the most common:

- The need for additional cash for have-to's (diapers, rent, tuition, bills, etc.) or want-to's (vacation, gifts, clothing, charity, etc.).

- Proximity to young children, aging parents, and other home-based duties.

- Escaping from a long commute, a bad boss, or annoying coworkers.

- Distraction from a life crisis like a divorce or the death of a parent.

- A desire to remain productive and intellectually stimulated.

- A sense that you're falling behind other women who have a job and connections in the outside world.

- A desire to achieve more control over your life.

- A desire to help other people, or make a professional contribution to an organization you care about.

- The need to save money on office space for an already thriving business.

See yourself in several of these? You may, or you may have very different reasons for considering a change. Take the time to think through *your* motivations—not those that reflect the wishes of your family or of anyone else. Write down your top five reasons and keep them close for a few days. You'll probably edit the list several times before you feel really good about it.

Assess Your Assets

Now that you've examined your personal work style and some of your motivations, the next step in determining your readiness is to assess your assets. Specifically, let's look at the hard and soft skills you've acquired over the years.

Hard skills are the ones you might typically list on a résumé or CV—abilities you learned in school or acquired through professional experience. Examples of hard skills include:

- You're bilingual in Spanish or another language.

- You're a whiz at Microsoft Excel.

- You're an efficient bookkeeper, experienced with QuickBooks.

- You bake fantastic cupcakes and your buttercream frosting is heavenly.

- You're an extremely fast and accurate typist.

- You're great at Internet research.

- You're a certified Pilates instructor.

- You've got ten years of experience in home inspection.

You get the idea. Hard skills are the credentials and abilities that set you apart. When creatively harnessed, it's that stuff that just might help you develop a rewarding at-home position, or perhaps even launch a successful business.

But hard skills themselves aren't enough. You also need the right soft skills to make it in your chosen field. These are the talents and qualifications that make you *you*. The ones your friends and family would use to describe you.

Here are some examples of soft skills:

- You are a world-class listener, known to be highly empathetic.

- You have a melodious voice and have always been great on the phone.

- You bounce back easily from disappointment, brush off, and get ready to try again.

- You're a quick learner and need little supervision.

- You're extremely easygoing and tend to avoid conflict.

- You've always had a knack for finding jobs for your girlfriends.

- You're a natural mediator.

Learn More About You

A relevant combination of hard and soft skills, as required by the position, is what any employer looks at when considering a candidate for a traditional job. But now, you're the boss—or at least you'd like to be. That means it's time to assess yourself as honestly and objectively as you can.

We've got an easy exercise to help. Get two pieces of paper (or, if you're like the mythical woman in the bulleted list above, make a quick spreadsheet with four columns). You want to end up with four spaces into which you can easily write or type. Name these:

- Soft skills, what I say about me

- Soft skills, what others say about me

- Hard skills, what I say about me

- Hard skills, what others say about me

Take some time to really think this through. Write down as many as you can under each category, then turn away from the exercise. Read on in this book, make some phone calls, or let it percolate until tomorrow. Come back to your lists one or two more times and keep adding, but don't delete anything. If it came to your mind once, it's worth leaving on the list.

If you're feeling ambitious, you might actually want to extend your inquiry to other people—friends, family, former supervisors who know you're planning on a change. Ask how they'd describe you and note their responses. Otherwise, try to see yourself from their perspective.

Now Play the Match Game

Keep the list handy. As you begin to hone in on what you would most like to do at home, you're going to match up the requirements of that job, business, or opportunity with your hard and soft skill set. As with the readiness quiz, you'll quickly see what you've got and what you need to get. Right there in black and white.

As you can see, making the lists is fairly easy to do. Then when you begin to align your skills with the requirements of the work life you'd like to live, it's pretty revealing. Consider Margaret, a fortysomething woman whose lists characterized her as a high-tech type who's very good with numbers and is more a loner than a social animal.

Not surprisingly, Margaret has spent twenty years in public accounting. Although she loved the work itself, she was never as comfortable with the client service part of her job. Margaret preferred to toil alone in her cubicle, turning out quality work with minimal human interaction. Her at-home ambitions may surprise you.

Margaret has had it with the world of numbers, she says. She's not interested in preparing tax returns from a quiet office in her finished basement as you might imagine (and as her skills would seem to indicate). Rather, she wants to start a small nursery because her unrequited love is gardening. Margaret has always had an amazing green thumb. She's long recognized that the time she spends planting and pruning is when she feels most productive and most complete.

After conducting some research, including conversations with the owner of her local greenhouse and a representative from a land-scape trade group, Margaret created a list of the skills, both hard and soft, she'd need to make it in the growing business.

Sure, there were some gaps she'd need to fill, like learning the ins and outs of identifying the right suppliers. But Margaret also found some surprising parallels between her current skills list and a career quite different from the one she'd known for two decades. She realized that her business knowledge (a hard skill) will make it easy for her to borrow money, keep the books, and manage her taxes, tasks most green-thumb types would find daunting.

Margaret also saw that her ability to work very intensely during busy season (i.e., the two months before April 15) was the same soft skill she'd need to face eighteen-hour days during spring planting season. Who knew that accounting and owning a greenhouse would require any similar skills?

Read the Tea Leaves

For women like Margaret who can envision what they want to do as at-home workers, the exercise is fairly linear. Her skill set matched up to some degree to what her dream job required. In order to fill in what's missing, Margaret is going to have to do some work.

But for other women, like thirty-year-old Kate, the list can help reveal a dream she may not have been aware of. We coach women all the time to take a nonlinear, nonthreatening look at their lives and their desired end result. Kate's list revealed that she had spent five years as a successful drug rep, helping to educate doctors and their staffs about new medicines, and encouraging them to purchase the lines her pharmaceutical company sells.

It was a satisfying run for Kate, who was always good in science and had even briefly considered medical school. But now she was the mother of two preschool daughters and needed to be closer to home. In reviewing her list of soft skills, Kate saw words that resonated—she was extremely patient, and she had always loved immediate feedback (the kind she felt after a big sale!).

Reviewing her spreadsheet, it dawned on Kate that she might like to tutor high school students in chemistry and biology. The subject matter was intuitive and familiar to her. As well, she had always loved the part of her job that involved "teaching" doctors and their staffs about new medical research, and drug interactions.

And heaven knows her patience would serve her well working with teens. Plus the ability to carve out a work schedule that meshed with her daughters' preschool and other activities was just what she had wanted.

Armed with the dream her lists helped her envision, Kate began to research tutoring. She joined a professional association, found some science tutors on a social networking website, and started to plan the next phase of her life.

Start to See Yourself in Her

Kate's experience reminds us how valuable it can be to untether ourselves from our experience and embrace a vision that, surprisingly, may not be that much of a stretch. Sometimes we tend to undervalue our assets, even selling ourselves short on what we are capable of becoming.

Yet we're really good at reinvention, and that's what realizing the work-at-home dream is really all about. We do it when we change our hairstyle or color, when we boldly decide to leave a dead-end relationship, or when we envision, and pursue, a brand-new career.

When it comes to becoming the successful at-home worker (employee, entrepreneur, contractor, etc.) some degree of reinvention is certainly required. Like Kate, you may discover that you are significantly lacking in some skills critical to your future and need to fill those gaps. For example, a successful transition from pastor to contractor (we know someone who did this beautifully!) might require six months of night courses at the local vocational or technical college.

For an attorney who wishes to take her job home, this might mean changing the area of the law in which she specializes to one that requires more research and brief writing and fewer out-of-town client meetings. Reinvention can mean retooling, relocating, researching, and, for many people, rethinking what they want out of work.

If you're lacking in what you think you'll need to succeed, you might also consider:

- Shadowing someone established in the field for several weeks to see what it's really like.

- Finding a business partner whose skills complement yours. In a mutually productive style, you learn from each other and eventually gain some of the skills you lack.

- Taking courses or reading books to master new skills and key knowledge.

- Faking it until you make it. Sometimes there's nothing left but to jump in with a healthy understanding of the risk you're facing and the knowledge that you have more energy and desire than your competitor.

Remember, it's just not enough to assume that you will make it and they will come. Promoting what you've made (packaged, written, cooked, built, or thought of) is enormously important to your success. Without the ability to sell your offering, it's unlikely that you'll make a go of it.

 **ACTION STEPS**

You've covered a lot of ground at this point and you should congratulate yourself. Our goal was to get you to begin thinking about what it means to work from home and to assess your readiness, motivation, and the skills you'll need to get there.

Don't feel disappointed if you haven't yet got the exact job, niche, initiative, or opportunity in mind. You don't need to. You just need to feel that you're willing to take a good look at your situation and keep working to figure it out. The answer is out there. Taking the following action steps will help solidify your understanding and will lead you forward:

1. *Take the Readiness Quiz* and score yourself honestly based on the discussion that follows it.

2. *Assess your soft and hard skills* with an eye to your own view of yourself, *and* how you appear to others. Begin to envision how these skills dovetail with requirements of a field you may wish to enter.

3. *Weigh the plusses and minuses* of home-working by dividing a sheet of paper into two columns—*rewards and challenges.* Consider social connections you might lose, family time you might gain, wardrobe, freedom, discipline, isolation, technology-income, and your ability to be creative and entrepreneurial.

4. *Jot down five at-home scenarios that just might work for you.* Think big, even crazy. Put down whatever comes to mind: aesthetician . . . adventure travel planner . . . online blogger . . . author . . . high-tech troubleshooter, etc. Save the list—you'll need it in just a few chapters.

■ ■ ■

chapter three

Taking Your Current Job Home

It's 8:45 in the morning and your workday is about to start. Your real day started over three hours ago. Your husband is on a business trip, so when the alarm went off you showered, dressed, and made coffee and school lunches before waking the kids. You poured cereal and juice, left the dishes in the sink, and gathered kids, book bags, and briefcase for the morning commute. You dropped your third-grader off at a friend's house to wait for the school bus and your daughter at a sitter's home, before heading to the interstate where you knew you would race or crawl, depending on traffic, the twelve miles to your downtown office. It took fifty-five minutes. Not too bad. Some mornings it's an hour and a half.

It's not the job that's killing you; it's the schedule. You trained for this career: The job is satisfying and pays well. You enjoy most of your coworkers, although the interruptions make it hard to concentrate on big projects, like the one that is due on Friday. Thank heaven for laptops, right? You'll work some tonight after the kids are in bed. Waiting for the coffee in the break room to perk, you think—not for the first time—how much simpler life would be if you could just work someplace closer to your neighborhood. Someplace with fewer distractions. *Somewhere like home.*

Taking your job home doesn't have to be an impossible mission. Others looking for a better balance of work and life have found ways to do it. You can, too.

The Trends Are in Your Favor

Telecommuting, or teleworking, the practice of traveling to the office by way of telephone and Internet, has been growing steadily in this country and around the world.

These days, one can be in business anywhere, as long as there's a laptop, high-speed Internet access, and a phone to use. TelCoa, the Telework Coalition, conducted a telecommuting study in 2006; the coalition surveyed public- and private-sector companies representing more than 500,000 employees and almost 150,000 teleworkers and remote workers and found that working from home, a hotel room, or a car, is no longer a dream of the future, but part of the mainstream of the working world.

Working outside the office is common for a growing number of employees, and not just because it's more convenient for them.

More companies are sending workers home because they are seeing bottom-line benefits. As executives share word of successful teleworking plans with their counterparts in other companies, we're seeing initial resistance turn to growing support. Flextime, which can include working from home, is good for people and for business.

Having employees work out of the office means reducing

corporate office space and utility costs. It may even free up parking problems. When the market has more jobs than applicants, it allows companies to draw from a larger pool of workers, including people who live beyond a reasonable commute or in other cities.

A remote workforce can be an asset in emergency situations. After the 9/11 terrorist attack, Hurricane Katrina, and other disasters, companies found that workers in nonaffected areas could help keep the business going.

Bosses also report that teleworkers are often more loyal, less likely to change employers, and that they get more done. There's less turnover. In short, teleworkers are happier.

That's a no-brainer, right? Of course you'd be happier if you could sleep a little longer, skip the commute, lose the power suit (not to mention the dry-cleaning costs) and heels—and if you could keep your career and salary, while working closer to your family and your community. Clearly, it's time to ask to take your job home. Ah, there's the rub—you have to ask.

Sure that's scary, but not when you approach it as you would any business project. You break it into logical steps, gather information and resources, weigh the benefits and the costs, make a plan and stick with it until you get the desired result. The path is there—others have already blazed it. You just have to decide to hit the trail.

Envision Your Goal

Tiger Woods doesn't just grab a golf club, tee up a ball, and take a swing. If he played golf like that, who would have ever heard of him? Instead he carefully envisions each shot. He looks at the hole with the flag in the distance, takes in the lay of the land and the hazards, thinks about where the ball needs to go, and what he needs to do to get it there. He knows it's a combination of the right club, the right stance, and the right swing for this particular piece of ground before he ever steps up to the tee. And before he swings, he knows exactly what he wants. He wants that ball to go into that hole in as few strokes as possible.

Before you put your work-from-home ball in motion, you need to define your goal. Do you want to work out of the office a few times a week? Does the ability to alter your hours to avoid a difficult commute during rush hour appeal to you? What could you do with two extra hours if you weren't commuting? If you're thinking trips to the park with your toddler, preparing better meals, meeting friends for coffee, taking an aerobics class, volunteering at church—you're beginning to envision your goal. You want time to work and get more out of life.

On the other hand, would you miss the stimulation of working with other professionals? Remember in school when you thought missing a day of school was a treat? But when the novelty wore off, you found yourself missing your friends and wondering what they were doing. Would working from home a couple of days a week be a better option? It would take some of the pressure off, and still let you feel a part of the team. Could you afford to work part-time? Would you be willing to become an independent contractor to achieve your goals?

If working away from the office isn't possible, would it help your schedule and budget to work four longer days? An extra day off would mean one day less of child care and commuting expenses and one day more to help your parents, be with your kids, or pursue your hobbies.

Everyone wants work/life balance, but not everyone wants it the same way. Before you ask for a change, know what it should

Happy at Home

Jennifer Silver had worked in the executive search industry for twenty years and was very happy with her job as director of marketing for CT-Partners, a global executive search firm. "The office was located in Burlington, Massachusetts, about fifteen to twenty minutes from my home." Her commute to the office and to her four-year-old daughter's child care was reasonable.

When the company moved its office to downtown Boston, it became another story. "It was taking me anywhere from an hour to an hour and a half to get to work," she says. "Our mornings became a crazy rush to get out the door. I kept thinking if I left ten minutes earlier, it would decrease the commute, but nothing worked."

She tried to answer calls during the commute, but the cell phone service was sketchy at best in some areas. Dropped calls left her feeling frustrated and behind by the time she arrived at the office. "I felt like I was missing a lot of work time," she says, "and since so much of my job is conducted by phone, e-mail, and computer, or on out-of-town business trips, I decided to talk to my boss about working from home. We had been together long enough that he knew my work ethic. He knew he could trust me." She also knew she could trust herself. She was disciplined and self-directed enough to do the work at home.

Still, Silver credits much of her success to moving her job home with her going to her boss with a plan. "I offered him a solution, not a problem," says Silver.

Since she didn't need to be face-to-face with coworkers to conduct business, and frequently was out of the office for national and international travel anyway, she was able to show that she could effectively do business at home. Losing the three-hour commute would make her a more relaxed and available worker, she believed. "Before talking to my boss, I made sure this was really what I wanted," she says. Her request was approved.

Silver is very happy in her job and with her company. She has a home office space and works by phone and laptop. The company installed the office phone system at her residence. She's available by phone and e-mail, talks to her boss every other day, and goes into the office for meetings or when she feels like being social.

As she predicted, working from home has improved her work and her life. Instead of rushing out the door and fighting traffic in the morning, Silver takes her daughter to child care and is at her desk by 8:30 A.M. "I find that I look like. When you can picture your desired result—your hole in one—you're on your way home.

Plan Your Hike

If home is where you want to work, you'll need a strategy. Getting your company to say yes will take preparation, planning, and persistence. You don't just get up one morning and decide to hike the Appalachian Trail, figuratively speaking. You need to consider how you'll live in the great outdoors in different seasons and weather, how long it will take, and what you'll need for the journey. You have to collect maps, boots, a compass, sleeping bag, tent, food, and other things to make the trip possible.

You need to start training, unless you're in peak physical condition. You'll also need to cover the bases at home before you walk out the door, and line up help in case of an emergency. It's not a simple undertaking. Yet many people hike the Appalachian Trail every year—one step at a time.

---

get more work done when people aren't interrupting me, and I have more time to be creative and think about work projects now," she says.

By working longer hours, and getting more done, she's able to work a four-day week most weeks and save Mondays and weekends for her family. Combining work and home allows her to throw in a load of laundry or run to the store during the day. Knowing that her daughter is only ten minutes away gives her greater peace of mind. When she travels, her family takes care of her daughter.

"It's been a great move and my career has not changed," says Silver. "I'm in the right position, working for the right person, and in the right kind of company. Our CEO's assistant is now working from home three days a week and that arrangement is working well, too."

🪟 Home Helper

Any undertaking is less daunting when divided into manageable parts. The Appalachian Trail is about 2,118 miles long and includes more than 350 peaks over 5,000 feet high. Many hikers complete it in about five months by setting goals for how many miles they must walk each day. They may reward themselves after an arduous stretch with a night off the trail in a motel and a restaurant meal.

So before you share your big idea with your boss, do your homework. When you daydreamed about working from home, you may have thought about sleeping late and working in your pajamas while the baby slept peacefully at your side. That's a Kodak moment, but doesn't take into account that babies wake up, often crying! So let's lose some common misconceptions:

Myth #1: WORKING FROM HOME IS A PIECE OF CAKE.

You may be in the comfort of your home, but you're not on vacation. You're working. Sticking to a schedule will take dedication and a strong sense of professionalism. To be available to your boss and coworkers, you may need to keep normal business hours. If your work isn't time-bound and you're working nights and weekends to avoid child care costs, you're working two jobs.

Myth #2: YOU WON'T NEED CHILD CARE.

If you're handling customer calls and dealing with time-sensitive materials, you can't have distractions. A quiet space that allows for uninterrupted work is essential. You'll need child care for young ones, and probably an after-school program for school-age children. Of course, ditching the commute might eliminate some child-care time and costs. Your working from home could also impact others in your household, such as an elderly parent, a roommate, or a spouse who works from home.

Myth #3: ANYBODY CAN DO IT.

Not true. Home-based workers need to be technologically savvy, since they'll be connecting to the office through a computer. Those who are comfortable using a PC and can do basic trouble-shooting when problems arise will find the job easier. You also need to understand your job.

Myth #4: ALL PERSONALITIES CAN BE SUCCESSFUL AT HOME.

We all have ways and situations where we work best. A long-distance runner and a football player are both athletes, but their sports require different skills. At home, you'll be directing your own work so you need to like working independently. You need to be good at setting and meeting your own goals. If you're the outgoing type and used to a busy office, working at home may be too quiet, unstructured, and lonely. You may miss the banter of office friendships. If you live alone or have young kids and want adult interaction, the office may be more of a social outlet than you think.

Like any workplace, home has advantages and disadvantages. If you're ready to trade your fantasy for a real-world plan, grab your notebook and begin to consider these questions. You'll need a good strategy to achieve your goal:

- Is your job portable?

- What would you need to work from home?

- What makes this a great idea—for you and your company?

- Does your company have a teleworking policy?

- How will you ask your boss?

- Are you prepared to negotiate?

- What if she or he says no?

- How will you safeguard your career while working at home?

Explore these questions as fully as possible. Write out your responses and revisit them in a day or two.

Can You Do Your Job at Home?

How easily could you pack up your duties and daily activities and take them out of the office? If you're a retail sales clerk, a hotel receptionist, a bedside nurse, or a bank teller, you can forget working from home. Your work depends on face-to-face contact with customers, guests, patients, or clients. However, many jobs that once required a physical presence in the office no longer do so.

This is an information age, and thanks to advances in technology, information can be shared, transferred, and managed from almost anywhere. Many lawyers, paralegals, computer programmers, IT specialists, writers, graphic designers, business analysts, distance-learning teachers, translators, accountants, and mid-level managers can and do work from home.

Home Helper

If your job won't transfer home, think about adapting your skills to a different role. For instance, a hospital nurse could become a phone-advice nurse for an HMO or an insurance company. A medical receptionist could take courses in medical billing and coding and do her new job at home.

The Coworkers

You may be in an office surrounded by other employees, but working largely independently. How much of your work requires face time with other workers and how much is done through technology? How often do you have to attend meetings? Does your team always gather in a conference room, or are ideas and progress reports shared virtually through conference calls, instant messaging, or e-mail attachments? Do you eat lunch with colleagues? How often do you exchange work challenges, ask for advice, and trade ideas to help you do your job? How would you replace that interaction if you worked at home? In a global corporation, your teammates, and your boss, may be in other cities, or even countries.

If there are parts of your job that must be done in the office, could they be shifted to one or two days a week, freeing you to work from home the rest of the time? Could responsibilities be traded or shared with another worker? Are you doing things that are not in your job description that keep you tied to the office?

Why? In a trimmed-down office, it's not unusual for people to wear multiple hats. It might be time to re-evaluate your job duties. Don't expect to unload duties and take your job home. That's not realistic and may get you branded as a lone wolf and not a team player. But if you're doing more than required and could continue doing it at home, your boss might consider a request for a change in workplace or schedule easier to grant than a petition for more money. It's all about strategy, remember?

 ## Home Helper

Make a list of your past work successes and accomplishments, especially any contributions you have made that were above and beyond your job description. It will remind you of your own worth as a worker and add to your confidence. Having some ready examples of your work ethic, experience, and company loyalty come in handy when negotiating for a more flexible work arrangement.

The Boss

Consider how working from home will change your boss's job. Will it make it harder, easier, or different? Is her management style more hands on or hands off? Is she open or resistant to change? Do you have a good working relationship built on mutual trust? Have you been on the job long enough to prove that you're a valuable employee? Would your expertise and experience be hard to replace? Keep in mind that a solid performance record is an excellent bargaining chip. You may want to make yourself a list of work successes before making your request.

The Clients

Do you meet clients in your office? Could you just as easily meet them at their office, or over a business lunch—a lunch you could travel to from home? What is your primary method of communication with them? Might there be any concern on their part that you work from a different location from your colleagues? Would your availability to them and their access to you be altered in any way if you worked from home?

 Home Helper

Many condominiums, apartment buildings, and public libraries have conference rooms that residents can reserve for business meetings, which is a viable option if you don't want to meet clients at home or make the lengthier commute to your office.

Is training delivered in a classroom at the corporate office, or online? If you are in charge of training, how much of your time is actually spent instructing employees, and how much preparing course materials on your own?

Have you ever had to get work done at home due to a sick child or family emergency and found it easier than you thought? What made it possible, and are those resources still available?

By looking at all the ramifications of taking your job home—professional, practical, financial, and emotional—you can solve many issues ahead of time. You can also anticipate some of your boss's objections, and have responses ready.

Happy at Home

At first glance, it seemed like it would take a miracle to extricate Rachel Smith Kovarsky from her office one day a week. What it took was a little coaching from an expert to create a proposal that covered all the bases.

With three young children, and a full-time job as administrative assistant to the director of medical research at Rush University Medical Center in Chicago, Kovarsky felt like she was constantly "surviving on coffee."

She wanted to be able to work from home one day a week after her youngest baby was born, but didn't know how to ask. "I'm not only administrative assistant, I'm my boss's right hand and serve as office manager to our fifty-five-member department staff," says Kovarsky. "I support four other managers, order supplies, and keep office equipment up and running."

"I doubt I would have had the nerve to ask for what I really wanted without Tory Johnson's help. I really appreciated her advice," says Kovarsky. "I just needed one day when I wasn't running to school, to day care, to work, and could get a few things done at home. But I didn't want people to think I wasn't taking my job seriously. Tory gave me confidence and some good pointers." One was to think it through from her boss's side, to show him how this would make her a better, more productive employee.

Kovarsky figured out which was her boss's least busy day and suggested that one as her time at home. She reminded him of all the things that she did and assured him that her work could continue, with a desk, computer, printer, fax, and phone at home. Knowing his reluctance, she suggested a pilot program, a one-month trial period to test the plan.

Kovarsky contacted the hospital's technical staff to make sure she could access hospital systems. She borrowed a laptop from the office and answered questions by phone, e-mail, and instant messaging, while working on a major project, and using her breaks to do household chores. "Most people had no idea I was out of the office. I was accessible, responsive, and right on point," she says. "The next day I caught up with tasks that needed to be done on-site and the world didn't end because I was out of the office for one day. It was heaven being able to work and have a life!

"We haven't formalized the plan yet, but that will come. My boss sees that it's seamless—the work gets done—and we're both comfortable with it," says Kovarsky. "I believe that this is a benefit that complements traditional compensation packages because it allows good employees to achieve work/life balance." She's proud to be an innovator for her workplace.

Home Helper

You don't have to spend a lot of money, but by decorating your office to suit your taste and personality, you'll take greater pleasure and pride in working there. It's your career—don't settle for makeshift quarters. If the company doesn't reimburse you for furniture or DSL, you can deduct those items on your return at tax time.

Consider the costs of moving home. Companies that have a formal flexible-work program may pay for the office furniture and equipment you need. They may hook you up to the office network and provide a business phone line. Installing new equipment, adding software, or putting security systems into place will add start-up costs to your working-from-home proposition. Just as at the office, you'll need supplies, such as printer ink, paper, file folders, and pens. Companies who already have teleworkers will probably furnish them or allow you to expense these items.

If you're the working-from-home pioneer in your company, you'll need to negotiate who pays for the cost of doing business. If you already have high-speed Internet service and can access the company intranet from home, or if your company supplies you with a cell phone, the costs may be minimal.

Just because you're asking to move your location of work doesn't mean you must assume the entire financial burden of working from home. For example, let's say you're confident that your productivity will increase because working from home will save three hours of commuting time. You plan to devote some of that time to your work, which will produce strong results for your employer. In such a case, you can ask the boss to cover the monthly cost of a dedicated business phone line.

Think about all of the costs you might incur—from paper and printer cartridges to phone bills and Internet service. The more your company values you and your work, the more you'll be able to ask them to cover. Don't make the mistake of being shy or feeling like you're greedy, both of which are common among people asking to work from home. They're so grateful to be approved to change their location or schedule, so they don't feel entitled to ask for anything else. Not good! Once you've proven the advantages to working from home, you should have the confidence to ask for the company to pay for some or all of the tools you'll need.

You may need or want to change your child-care arrangements. If your children are in school, losing the commute may mean that you can put them on the bus yourself. You may also be able to take children later or pick them up earlier from a sitter, and have more time to spend with them. But if your sitter comes to the home or your child-care center is close to your office, you'll probably have to make adjustments. If you have teenagers, you'll need to set rules about interruptions and household noise during work hours.

Home Helper

A working-from-home mother can be a role model to children, showing them day-to-day how to balance work and play. For instance, if children do their homework while Mom works, then everyone can take a break together. Older children can learn responsibility by watching younger ones when Mom has a deadline to meet.

Defining Workplace Flexibility

There are many forms of flexible work options to consider:

Telecommuting: You work full-time from home, away from the corporate offices. You may even be in another city or state. You maintain regular working hours and all of your communication is handled remotely. You travel as needed for work to meet with clients, coworkers, and bosses.

Compressed workweek: Some employers—from retailers and grocery chains to banks and corporations—allow employees to work a compressed week. Instead of working five days for eight hours a day, for example, they'll work four days at ten hours each. This frees up one day each week to focus on personal/family needs or to save on child-care costs on that fifth day.

Altered workday schedule or flextime: In addition, some employers—including the federal government—will allow some employees to devise an alternative schedule for start and stop times. A mom who wants to see her child off to school can choose a later start time. She can put the kids on the bus herself, and save the cost of morning child care, but stays later.

This is also great if you live in a city with terrible traffic. Coming in an hour or two later could save you time and sanity. By avoiding the rush hour, you'll get to work faster and save that dead time on the road.

Vacation by the hour: This works well for workers paid by the hour. If they miss a shift, their pay is docked. It's also ideal for small businesses because it doesn't cost a penny to implement. For example, you need to take your child to the doctor. Instead of missing the entire shift, you'll take off the hour you need and then return to work. Your vacation time works like a debit account—you deduct the hours you needed to take.

This allows you to take care of family matters without missing a day's pay. The company benefits because it doesn't lose out on a full day of your productivity.

Eleventh-hour understanding: Another form of flexibility relates to the management style of your boss. Some people can call at 8:00 A.M. to say they are running late and the boss allows them to make up the time on their own terms. This means employees benefit from peace of mind and don't have to fret over sick kids, emergency eldercare demands, or other unexpected distractions. An understanding boss is often the most beneficial form of flexibility for many people.

Create a Win-Win Scenario

You know how working from home will improve your life. When we speak around the country, we hear from thousands of workers who want flexibility for many different reasons. One wants to take three-day motorcycle trips with her spouse, another wants to get her MBA, while another needs to be more available to an aging parent. Some common benefits employees cite are:

- More time for things that matter to them

- Reduced travel time and costs

- Less stress in combining work and family

- More control over job and career

- No longer have to miss school or community events

- Can further education

- Can focus on work with fewer interruptions from coworkers

- Can remove themselves from office gossip and politics

- Retain benefits and advancement opportunities

- Keep job skills sharp

If, however, you want to improve your odds of getting approval—downplay the benefits to you, and focus on those to the company. When Jennifer Silver pointed out that she could be working earlier each morning instead of spending time on the highway to Boston, it made sense to her boss. He thought she would be more productive if she was relaxed and focused. He was right. Studies of corporate teleworking programs find that the productivity of at-home workers increases between 10 and 40 percent.

Most companies find that workplace flexibility increases

Happy at Home

The first time that sixteen women from the billing department of a Dallas doctor's office asked to work a compressed workweek, they did it verbally, and were denied. Their casual method of asking showed they hadn't put much thought into it and management didn't take it seriously.

After coaching from Tory Johnson, they came back with a formal proposal a year later. They had a common goal, which they explained clearly. Because of long commutes, a desire to pursue personal hobbies, and the demands of family life, they all wanted to work four days and have three-day weekends. They realized that everyone taking work home one day a week was not a workable option given confidentiality concerns regarding sensitive patient records.

They proposed covering the bases of a five-day office with fewer workers, and better communication between workers, thus allowing some to take off Monday and others Friday. They showed their commitment to the job by what they were willing to do in exchange for a four-day week. They had already brainstormed the possible objections and included solutions in their document—and this time the answer was yes!

employee morale and improves motivation. Knowing that their companies trust them to work on their own, employees have greater confidence and company loyalty.

According to the Families and Work Institute's ongoing National Study of the Changing Workforce, flexible and effective workplaces benefit everyone. Employees gain from a workplace that respects the fact that they have a job and a personal life. Employers benefit from having more engaged employees who demonstrate higher levels of job satisfaction. Satisfied employees work better, stay longer, and may make fewer demands on health-care benefits, because they are less stressed. Tell a company you can save money on employee health premiums, and you've got their attention. Those costs rise every year.

Even more pertinent to the bottom line, companies with tele-working programs save dollars on facility and utility costs. Suppose your division needs another worker and space is tight. Your office would be available if you went home to work.

Asking the Boss

You've thought it through, done your research, and know your plan has merit—now all you have to do is ask the boss. Don't do it casually, and certainly not when you're stressed out by the commute or a problem at home. If you're asking for a serious change, write a formal proposal. It will get more consideration than an offhand suggestion and complaint. You need to:

Put it in writing. A formal written document not only exemplifies the seriousness and professionalism of your request, it also allows the boss to digest it as many times as he'd like. Since he may have to seek input or approval from others, your written document avoids the risks that he'll miscommunicate (even inadvertently) your wishes.

Explain what you want. Be specific. One day at home, two days at home, teleworking full-time, leaving two hours early each day, and making up that time by working after dinner.

Show how it can work. Cover the hardware and software issues and how they can be overcome to keep work flowing. If you're already communicating often through e-mail or phone, that part of your job won't change. Offer to come in for meetings, or to help with unexpected crises. This is a perk, so admit your willingness to be flexible and to put in the extra effort to make it work. Remind him of your past performance appraisals that show you know your job and work well without supervision.

Make it a win-win. Tell why the arrangement will benefit you, but also how it will benefit the company. You get to go home. He gets a more productive, focused employee, and is able to keep your years of experience on the team. That beats turnover cost. After allowing a young mother to work from home, one Atlanta law firm found that she had more billable hours because she wasn't commuting or chatting at the coffee machine, like her colleagues. They got to keep an experienced and loyal lawyer, and all it cost was a scanner so that she could scan legal briefs into her computer.

Go green. Companies are increasingly environmentally conscious and are adapting a variety of ways to go green. Not only does this play into their roles as good corporate citizens, but being environmentally friendly is also often incorporated in their recruitment and retention strategies. Allowing employees to work from home is one aspect to these policies. So if you know it's an area of sensitivity and concern for your employer, you'll want to tout this benefit in your proposal.

Anticipate the opposition. Think of the reasons why your boss might say no. Among the possible reasons:

- It's not company policy.

- If I let one, everyone will want to do it.

- I need face time with you to discuss ideas, etc.

Include counterarguments. For instance, many companies are creating flexible-schedule policies and seeing real benefits. Other people like coming to the office, don't have small children, and live closer—so not everyone wants to work at home. And you're willing to come to the office for meetings. A question-and-answer section or bulleted points included in your written proposal will make this key information easy to read and digest.

Propose benchmarks. Show how your work can be measured, even if you aren't at your desk. Your boss will have to answer to your productivity. Make it easy for him to know what you are doing. How will you evaluate your communication? Will colleagues get to weigh in on the arrangement?

Suggest a trial period. Your boss may be more willing to try a three-month experiment than a permanent change. This gives you both time to negotiate the details and work out the bugs.

Be confident and enthusiastic. Just because you're ready to start this new arrangement tomorrow, doesn't mean the boss is ready to commit. You like your job and the company and you believe that granting this request will make your work even better. That's the main message you want to deliver. You want to avoid painting a scenario that would question your commitment to this job and your responsibilities if your proposal is for any reason rejected.

Don't expect an immediate answer. Your boss may need to talk to his or her boss, to human resources, and to the technical department to make a decision. Be sure to ask when you can discuss the proposal again. Establishing a time frame for further conversation will help you to manage your expectations.

Expect to negotiate. Know what you are willing to give in order to get what you want. You may get the two days at home, but have to pay for DSL yourself. Or the company might agree to send you home full-time as an independent contractor. That would mean loss of benefits. If you have a spouse with health insurance, you might want to consider it. If you're a single mother, this probably isn't an affordable arrangement. Of course, you could get an unqualified, "Yes, we're so glad you thought of this," but it doesn't hurt to think about other possibilities.

Building Your Case

A work-from-home request is a business decision and requires you to build a business case for it. Here's how to lay the groundwork.

- Be a strong performer on the job. Flextime is an accommodation, not an entitlement. Slackers won't get the benefit of the doubt. Being a good worker will greatly improve your chances of getting a green light.

- Talk to your human resources department to see if a flexible work schedule policy is in place. If so, ask to speak to employees and managers who are participating. Gather some firsthand tips on how well it's working, and ask about problems you and your boss should avoid.

- Research teleworking on the Internet and gather some statistics to impress your boss. (See resources for suggested sites.)

- Research the competition. Ask your industry colleagues about their company policies and best practices. Flexibility is a highly desired benefit, and one your company may want to explore in order to attract and retain the best and brightest workers.

- If others share your desire to work from home and you can establish a common goal—join forces. There's safety and leverage in numbers.

Flexible Work Proposal

We've created a template for a flexible work proposal. Use it to help build the case and the documentation you'll need to get from here to there.

MEMO

TO: (First and last name of your boss and title)
FROM: (Your first and last name and title)
DATE: (Today's date)
SUBJECT: Flexible Work Proposal

I'd like to request a meeting to discuss my proposal for moving from my current full-time, onsite work schedule to a more flexible arrangement. I look forward to sharing with you my thoughts about a schedule I believe would be equally beneficial for the company and for me.

As you know, I currently work [fifty] hours in the office each week. I am proposing a shift that would involve working from my home office [two] days a week. I value my role here and I look forward to continuing to contribute to the company's success. Moving to a flexible schedule would help me remain productive while staying responsive to the needs of my family.

As you will see in this document, I've given a great deal of thought to this proposal, which I hope you will review with equal consideration.

Thanks very much in advance. I hope to hear from you soon about a possible day and time to meet and discuss. As always, I appreciate your support.

Proposed plan of action: In this section, you offer details about the specific job tasks you anticipate doing from home and why, plus the tasks you will perform from the office setting and why. Present the material in terms of value for your team and employer, with a lesser emphasis on how it will help you personally.

Communication: This is where you lay out a detailed plan for how you will remain in touch with your boss, your team, and your clients. You might include a request for a Blackberry or other PDA, whose cost you share with the company. You may wish to propose a regular daily conference call at a set time. Or possibly a weekly report on your activities, sales calls, and other tasks.

Benefits: This is a critically important section in which you clearly define the benefits of a flexible arrangement. If necessary, review the firm's mission statement and state your case in a way that corresponds with it. Think in terms of productivity, focus, uninterrupted work time, and other plusses. Be sure to list the advantages for you, as well.

Cultural issues: In this section, you address the company's culture—what makes it unique and how those characteristics work in favor of a flexible working arrangement. For example, you may note that the company was named an employer of choice by a prestigious publication. Explain how establishing a flexible work option reinforces that image internally and within the larger community.

Trial period: If you think you need some leverage, propose a trial period at the end of which you, your boss, and perhaps the head of HR agree to come together to assess the arrangement. Take careful notes during the trial period and prepare a succinct, but excellent report.

Evaluation process: Your proposal should include a detailed evaluation process such as quarterly reports submitted by you and reviewed by your supervisor and HR. You should be mindful that being a pioneer has its challenges. You may have to be the "poster child" for flexible scheduling to pave the way for others to follow. Stay the course and the results will be yours to enjoy.

What If the Answer Is NO?

If your boss isn't interested in your proposal, resist the urge to appear deflated and angry. That sends a message of concern that you might start to slack off on your responsibilities. Instead, calmly ask a few key questions:

- Would you be able to explain to me why there is hesitation about the proposal?

- Are there some specific things I can do to make the proposal more appealing?

- Are there other people within the company that you'd like me to speak to directly to address their questions and concerns?

- Would there be a good time to revisit this issue?

- Is there any additional research or information I could provide for you?

Change takes time and patience and you must have both—along with the ability to bounce back from initial rejection. Proper perseverance will help you get through this time.

If the answer is a total negative, as in "no way, not ever," it's time to reassess your options. Maybe you could move closer to the office or job-share. Or you could take your considerable skills and ingenuity to a more enlightened employer. There are plenty of progressive companies that have embraced flexible work programs. Check out:

- *Fortune* magazine's 100 Best Companies to Work For; Money.CNN.com/magazines/fortune

- The Great Place to Work Institute best companies lists; GreatPlaceToWork.com

- *Fortune* magazine's America's Most Admired Companies; Money.CNN.com/magazines/fortune/mostadmired

- *Working Mother* magazine's 100 Best Companies for Working Mothers; WorkingMother.com

- AARP's Best Employers for Workers over 50; AARPMagazine.org

- The *Information Week 500*, which names innovative users of information technology; InformationWeek.com

- *Forbes* magazine's 200 Best Small Companies; Forbes.com/lists

- *ComputerWorld*'s 100 Best Places to Work in IT; ComputerWorld.com

- *Black Collegian* magazine's Top 100 Diversity Employers; Black-Collegian.com

Home Helper

Some agencies within the federal government have a progressive approach to teleworking and initiatives to send employees home. Visit the Telework Exchange, a public-private partnership, at teleworkexchange.com.

Use your business and personal network in your job search. Talk to friends, family, and business associates about their company's attitude on flexibility. Tell people your goals: You want a job that fits your skills and career direction, and a company that will appreciate your ability to work from home. Fortunately, those opportunities are growing every day. Ultimately, you shouldn't be discouraged if your company or boss doesn't embrace your plan, because there are plenty of other options.

If the Answer Is YES!

Woohoo! Your proposal was approved. You did it. But now there's other work to be done to ensure a smooth transition to your new schedule or work style. Depending on the size of your company and the nature of your work, you'll want to touch base with several people about the next steps. Among those to consult: your boss and any other managers, the HR department, coworkers, clients, and colleagues with whom you work closely. Agree on a start date with your direct manager and determine together how to communicate this new arrangement with everyone who needs to know. It's important to manage the expectations of all of these people so there's no misunderstanding about your commitment to your job. You'll want to address:

- Contact information: How will you be reached? Is there a new phone or fax number? What is the new address to which you'll need materials sent? Does your e-mail address remain the same?

- Hours of work: Are you reachable on certain days and times? Are there any times that are now off limits?

- Methods of communication: How will you stay in touch with everyone so you don't miss out on things you might've learned by being physically in the office? Do you want to arrange weekly conference calls? Would you liked to be copied on e-mails that you previously didn't receive? Will you make visits regularly to the office?

Your boss isn't the only one you must impress with this new arrangement. He or she will no doubt hear from colleagues if they believe you're now difficult to reach or you're not as involved and on the ball as you once were. Everyone you work with has the ability to influence the success or failure of this new arrangement.

If you have direct reports, work together to determine how you'll provide direction, coaching, and feedback from a distance. Reiterate that your commitment to the position and your expectations of them have not changed; only the location of your desk is now different. Map a plan for how often and by what means you'll communicate.

Offer the courtesy of an update to people who are indirectly impacted. For example, you might work with a client or colleague in another state who has no idea where you physically work. Instead of letting that person hear from someone else that you don't work in the office anymore, which can sometimes imply that you've "checked out," give that person a heads-up. You might send an e-mail saying, "Even though we don't get to see each other, I want you to know that I've been approved for a flexible work arrangement that now allows me to work from home. That will not change my availability or accessibility to you. Here's the new number to reach me; my e-mail address remains the same, as does my commitment to our professional relationship."

Refer often to the benchmarks you proposed so you're aware of how you'll be evaluated, especially when it comes time to extend the trial period or make the arrangement permanent.

Managing Your Career
from Home

Whether you achieve your goal with your current company, or find a new employer, the responsibility is on you to make working from home work. It's your job to make sure people know that you are meeting your obligations. Stay on the company radar. You don't want to be "out-of-sight, out-of-mind," and passed over for career advances and plum assignments. Here's how to attend to business from home:

- Build a good remote communications system by making and keeping regular phone appointments with your boss to discuss your work. Talk about problems and successes.

- Get reports and other materials in on time or ahead of schedule.

- Stay in touch with coworkers by phone and e-mail. Be a team player. Ask to be copied on department e-mails and included in social functions. Read the company newsletter and intranet. Stay abreast of employee news.

- Ask your boss about new initiatives or projects on the horizon. Offer to help brainstorm, be part of the team, or troubleshoot problems. Point out assignments that fit your skills and interests—ask for the projects you really want.

- If there's a company mentoring program, get involved. You don't have to be onsite to give valuable advice and encouragement. You can use the phone, e-mail, or instant messaging and meet for an occasional lunch.

- Volunteer for responsibilities or assignments that will stretch your skills. Ask for appropriate training or continuing education. Attending classes at the office for a few weeks could be worth it if it puts you on the management track.

- Make it known that you want to keep growing and advancing with the company. Always show enthusiasm for your job.

- Keep up career affiliations. Network and attend professional organizations to keep up with industry trends.

Making a Smooth Transition

Even though you wanted it and asked for it—working from home can be an emotional adjustment. Your working family was a big part of your day.

Tend to relationships: You may encounter jealousy from coworkers who think that being at home isn't really working. Remember your early fantasies? Let them know that it's not all leisurely lunches and watching soap operas at your end. You're still working, only with a new set of challenges. Be honest. Tell them you miss their input and value their friendship now more than ever. Show interest in their lives and work. They may even meet you halfway for lunch.

Set workable boundaries: When you were out of the house, you weren't available. Now that you're home, a friend may drop by for coffee or invite you to a sale. You'll have to explain gently, but firmly, that this is work time. You can't shop or watch little Jimmy while she runs an errand—you've got a conference call. For persistent pests, caller ID can be a lifesaver.

Maintain contacts: Keeping up your professional network, participating in industry associations, and attending conferences will keep your skills sharp. Read trade publications in your field.

 Action Steps

1. *Keep a log for a week and see where your time goes.* Do you wonder why you can't get everything done? You may be able to make some adjustments, or you may see why you need to ask to work from home.

2. *Figure out your average commuting time.* Now make a list of all that you could do with that extra two hours. Let your imagination run wild. Think about what you could save in gas and car maintenance. Think about what you're missing when you're stuck in traffic—your kids' ball games, an exercise class, trying a new recipe for dinner. Asking your boss to work from home takes courage. Break out your list whenever you need motivation.

3. *Take a close look at your job.* Could you do it at home? Are there issues to overcome? What three steps can you take to start working on them?

4. *If you don't have a home office, find a space for one.*

5. *Think about the best ways to approach your boss to achieve your goals.*

6. *Make a timetable for researching, writing, and delivering a written work-from-home proposal to your boss.* Set realistic goals and stick to them.

■ ■ ■

chapter four

Fill an Existing Need

Good news! Your decision to enter the from-home workforce comes at possibly the best time in history. That's because businesses—lots of them—are actually *looking for* home workers.

This means abundant opportunities to work for existing businesses as an employee, contractor, or freelancer. You may have start-up costs to cover training and materials, but you don't have to come up with a new idea or run a large business. You can just work hard, stay focused, and make money.

Business owners are realizing the benefits of flexible work options and are starting to send the trend mainstream. From the federal government to Wall Street and back to Main Street, employers are paying attention because feedback from workers indicates the growing desire for varied work styles. To lure the best talent and to retain those people, companies will have to adapt to workforce demands. For you, it means the possibility of greater convenience, more money, and a lifestyle-friendly work style.

As you'll see, good opportunities are no longer limited to brick-and-mortar offices or call centers, nor must they be outsourced overseas. There are lots of new and exciting possibilities out there.

Plusses for Them

An increasing number of companies now realize that working at home can be as valuable for them as it can be for you. One of the biggest advantages is retention. Business owners are seeing that saying yes to working at home—some or all of the time—is a key strategy to retain competent female employees who demand, and deserve, flexibility.

Greater efficiency is another employer plus. Most employers report the shift to working at home results in a boost in productivity for businesses and individuals that use it.

Other benefits include:

- The ability to attract a more diverse workforce.

- A larger pool of interested, motivated applicants.

- Reduced expenses related to infrastructure, benefits, etc.

- Less employee stress and burnout.

It's a Workers' Market out There

Filling an existing need means aligning your skills and desires with available opportunities. In a sense, it's the opposite of becoming an entrepreneur. Work is funneled to you as an independent contractor, freelancer, or, depending on the organization, as an actual employee. When you fill an existing need, you don't own the concept and you don't own the business. Your job is to do what you do best to help somebody else's business succeed.

In exchange, you make money conveniently and often on your schedule. You're also relieved of the burdens of daily business operations, like meeting payroll, paying taxes, and figuring out how to stay ahead of the competition.

Online Job Boards Are a Good Place to Start

You'll find loads of at-home postings on all the major job boards, including HotJobs.com, CareerBuilder.com, and Monster.com. SimplyHired.com and Indeed.com compile available positions from a variety of sources. When searching, the trick is to include the words "virtual," "home-based," "telework," or "telecommute."

TheLadders.com focuses on positions paying more than $100,000 annually and requires a monthly fee to join. It offers a wide range of senior-level positions from marketing to sales, technology to finance. You can also promote your own skills and abilities on sites such as Elance.com, Odesk.com, Sologig.com, and Guru.com, where employers search to find good talent. Craigslist.com and Backpage.com both post local listings.

As with any advertised opportunity, be sure to do your homework to determine if a job you see online is right for you. That means talking to a person, not just relying on an e-mail exchange to learn in-depth about the requirements, challenges, and potential earning power. Beware of postings that promise big bucks for minimal effort. If it were that easy, we'd all be working in those jobs!

Proceed with Caution

Whether you find your job on an online board, in the newspaper, or from a personal referral, don't underestimate the commitment. Some people mistakenly believe that working from home is necessarily easier than working in a traditional environment. In fact, the opposite can be true, especially at the beginning.

As people get accustomed to balancing home and family life and as employers get comfortable with the setup, you may have to go above and beyond to justify the change. Also be aware that when you join an organization from home you may need to put up money to cover training, equipment, and materials. And depending on your status, you may not have much in the way of a formal guarantee or job security.

This can be worrisome, even deal-killing, for some people. But others accept it as part of the risk, one they're willing to take in exchange for freedom, convenience, proximity to home, and all the other reasons that lead you there.

Job Shop 'til You Drop

We've identified some of the hottest categories and the best companies in the country currently hiring at-home workers. But they represent just the tip of the iceberg. Your search should be broad and thoughtful. Give this the time it needs and your patience will pay off.

Medical Coding and Billing Specialist

Medical coders and medical billers collaborate to ensure that healthcare providers are paid for their services. Coders analyze the documentation provided to assign diagnostic and procedural codes. This information must be properly recorded for the reimbursement process. Coders may also get involved in medical research and statistics in an effort to properly assign reimbursement codes.

Medical billers prepare and submit claims to insurance companies or the government, primarily Medicare, in order to obtain payment for services provided by a health-care professional.

Although entry-level work does not require higher education, most employers require specialized training in coding and billing. To allow work at home, most employers insist on prior experience.

Got these?
Qualifications for medical coders and billers include the following:

- Experience and/or training in the field.

- Detail orientation and an ability to persevere in order to obtain needed information.

- Patience and problem-solving skills.

Contact these:
Check out the opportunities at MedQuist.com and PrecyseSolu tions.com, among other similar resources.

Medical Transcription Specialist

The medical services industry is enormous and growing. Medical transcription is a specialized field in which specialists interpret and transcribe dictation by doctors and other health-care professionals. The information is usually recorded onto digital voice-processing systems or tape.

If you're experienced in the field and want to work at home, there are some excellent opportunities available. Some employers require that medical transcriptionists have in-hospital or in-office experience before they work from home. Bottom line—this is a tough field for beginners to break into. (If you seek training in the field, visit the website of the Association for Healthcare Documentation Integrity, AHDIonline.org).

The pay range varies widely from about $10 per hour to $25 or more depending on experience. Without prior experience, it's almost impossible to get hired at home.

Got these?

Qualifications and requirements for medical transcriptionists include:

- Up-to-date computer, high-speed Internet access, a landline, and most likely a headset and foot pedal to operate transcription equipment.

- Specialized software you may be required to purchase.

- Training and industry experience.

- Ability to meet strict deadlines.

- Good communication skills and the ability to multitask.

Contact these:

In addition to the major online job boards, visit MedQuist.com, PrecyseSolutions.com, and MedWord.com.

Technical Support Specialist

If you're an experienced information technology professional who enjoys troubleshooting, you may be able to land a job providing technical support via phone, online, or in person.

Depending on the company, you may be hired as an independent contractor or as an employee. But regardless of the setup, you'll be able to set your own hours and apply a much-needed skill. Expect to earn between $10 and $50 per hour and to work at least twenty hours per week.

Got these?

In order to be seriously considered for a remote technical-support position, you'll need the following:

- An up-to-date computer, high-speed Internet access, and a landline.

- Significant experience in technical support, including certifications or related proof of skills.

- A can-do attitude and problem-solving skills.

- Patience for customers who are less technically savvy.

Contact these:

Check out GeeksOnTime.com, GeekSquad.com, Computer Assistant.com, PlumChoice.com, SupportFreaks.com, and Support .com. More services are cropping up all the time, both locally and nationally, so a search engine and job board will turn up more results in this category.

Telemarketer

If annoying calls from telemarketers are one of your pet peeves, consider becoming one yourself and change the image. Many businesses, nonprofits, and political organizations outsource their cold-calling campaigns to third parties. Those firms hire full- and part-time people, many who work from home to place calls.

The purpose of the calls varies. You could be hired to persuade those you call to book an appointment, make a donation, or agree to try a product or service. Some telemarketing calls are to collect debts.

Typically, telemarketers earn an hourly base pay (on average between $6 and $15) plus performance-based commission. While some training is provided, applicants should have some experience in high-quality customer service and/or cold calling.

Got these?

At-home telemarketers require the following, but, like all fields, the specifics will vary by company:

- An up-to-date computer, high-speed Internet access, and a landline.

- A quiet place to work without interruption or background noise.

- A pleasant phone voice and manner.

- Patience with prospects who may get annoyed that you've called them at home, or who don't wish to hear from the organization you represent.

- Prior customer service or sales experience is preferred in many cases.

Contact these:
Among firms that hire telemarketers are Telereach.com, Intrep
.com, and West.com. Find others by searching "telemarketing
opportunities" on big job boards and search engines.

Tutor

Organizations and educational service providers are turning to
online tutors for a number of reasons, primarily client convenience. The field is relatively new and quite promising. Depending
on the employer, it's open to college graduates or current students
at accredited schools with experience in English, math, science,
social studies, and languages. You can bypass these requirements by
working on your own. You'll also earn much more per hour as an
in-person versus online tutor.

   Rates start at $10 an hour and higher; you'll be expected to

Happy at Home

"Think outside the house and virtually anything is possible. One of the
smartest things you can do when running a home-based business is to create a virtual team. My company, UptownScoop.com, a daily e-note that
keeps busy women in business in the know about what's hip, hot and trend-
worthy relative to their careers, has employees—creative writers, IT support,
ad sales and more—all working from their homes in cities across the country.
Thanks to technology, we are all seamlessly—and virtually—working toward
the common goal of keeping smart women connected to smart resources.
The very best employees are not necessarily just in your neighborhood. More
likely they are in some other city, state or even country. When you work from
home, you are perfectly positioned to build a virtual team that includes the
smartest people, regardless of their location. Think big, think outside the
house, think smart—and virtually anything is possible."

—Lynne Fair Homrich, Georgia

work from five to thirty hours per week. The work is highly flexible as most arrangements are for weekly tutoring sessions of one to two hours.

Some tutors work regularly with private and public schools, even becoming the preferred tutor for a particular school. This can be a great way to increase your hours and earn a reputation with parents. It may mean operating out of the school, instead of home, for a certain number of hours per week.

Intense competition for top colleges has boosted the market for college preparatory and SAT/ACT tutoring. The Kaplan organization is among those often hiring both onsite and online tutors.

Got these?
Qualifications for tutors include the following:

- A college degree or current enrollment.

- An ability to work with students of all ages.

- Patience and problem-solving skills.

- Transportation to and from assignments for off-line clients.

Happy at Home

"I handle inbound phone orders and outbound call verification. Being an independent contractor means I provide services for virtual companies under a contract agreement. I schedule my own hours and maintain my own equipment. I can make as much as I want, when I want, and I am responsible for my own taxes. I am my own boss. I get paid by the minute for one position and by the hour with the other. I have made as much $1,200 in one pay period. I now enjoy life and time with my family and indeed I have found 'The Dream Job.'"

—Carolyn Mason, Pennsylvania

Contact these:
There's a lot of information and opportunity online at Tutor.com, TutorVista.com, ASAPTutor.com, Kaplan.com, GrowingStars.com, and SmarThinking.com. You can find others by searching under "online tutors."

Virtual Assistant (VA)

Wanted—proven self-starter with a solid administrative background. If this sounds like you, there may be a job as a virtual assistant in your future. This exciting (and exploding) field is made up of administrative professionals who work from their home offices, providing professional support services to clients via phone, fax, and Internet-based technology.

According to Tawnya Sutherland, founder of a virtual assistant networking association, VAnetworking (VANA), typical tasks might include: phone answering, e-mail management, dictation, database management, and word processing. Depending on the industry, more technical or content-driven skills may be required.

Sutherland, a tireless advocate for a field she loves and has succeeded in for more than a decade, runs an info-packed website at VAnetworking.com. She offers free site memberships as well as fee-based memberships with additional benefits. Members get insider information and the opportunity to network with other VAs. Members can buy and sell used office equipment, learn how to market themselves, get tips on website design, and much more.

The site also has lots of content for nonmembers, including information about qualifications and ways to avoid common pitfalls.

VAs typically earn between $10 and $75 per hour. Many VAs have multiple clients throughout the country or across the world.

Sutherland recommends working on a retainer basis. For example, if you are retained to work for ten hours, you may wish to create an incentive by offering a discount off the hourly fee. Seek payment or even a deposit in advance, she recommends. This is a hedge against getting stiffed by an unknown client and it keeps your cash flowing rather than waiting for payment after the fact.

Got these?
To offer your services as a virtual assistant to a current employer, or to market yourself to a new business, here's what you need:

- An up-to-date computer, high-speed Internet access, and a landline.

- A quiet, dedicated workspace that's not the kitchen table.

- Administrative experience and/or training.

- A pleasant phone voice and manner.

- The ability to multitask whether you're working for one or more employers.

- Strong organizational skills.

No experience? No problem.
Women who would like to become a VA but do not have administrative experience might consult AssistU.com. President Stacy Brice has developed a twenty-week training course, which requires a financial investment.

There's a sliding-fee structure based on the type of course work and method of study—from small group to private lessons.

Like VAnetworking.com, AssistU has plenty of free information.

There's a private members-only area with additional content. Membership is free to those who graduate from the AssistU training. The site also includes a referral service.

On the double!

Team DoubleClick (TeamDoubleClick.com) is one of the largest virtual staffing agencies, with 26,000 placements. Virtual assistants can expect to make about $10 to $15 per hour, more if they have specialized skills. They can work as few or as many hours as they like. Training is done by self-study and is relatively quick for qualified applicants. Applicants should have good typing and office skills and a positive, can-do attitude, which can be even more important than years of experience.

Why Hire a VA?

Wondering why clients might hire you to work from home as an administrative assistant? Here are some of the benefits to them that you'll want to keep top of mind when pitching your services *(Adapted with permission, Virtual Assistant Networking Association)*:

- Clients save money on office space, computers, and other equipment. They pay only for the time a VA actually works.
- There's no need to coordinate work schedules; simply send off the work to be done with a due date.
- Clients pay no health insurance, vacation pay, or employer wage reductions because VAs usually assume their own overhead costs.
- VAs are familiar with tools and technology and require limited on-the-job training.
- VAs know how business operates because they run their own businesses.
- There's no downtime related to commuting as VAs work from their home offices.
- Client information flow is protected through confidentiality agreements.

Contact these:

VAnetworking.com, AssistU.com, and TeamDoubleClick.com all offer details about the work of virtual assistants, plus help identify prospects and get necessary training. GetFriday.com is a concierge service based in India, but its website offers lots of ideas and inspiration about the array of services you could offer on your own.

Virtual Concierge

Not so long ago, the term *concierge* referred only to a member of a hotel staff who handles special guest services or someone in charge of the entrance of a building. Today, the concept and the demand are expanding beyond the hospitality industry.

Concierges work in every type of business. Google offers its busy staffers access to concierge services to minimize the stress of personal errands and chores. Their job is to handle phone, e-mail, and online customer inquiries for services ranging from making dining suggestions and reservations to planning a vacation for busy professionals. Some businesses have found that it's more effective to hire a concierge service to help busy employees get things done than to give them the time off to do the chores themselves.

VIPdesk (VIPdesk.com) is a leading supplier of concierge programs and services. The company's clients are executives and employees of some of the world's leading businesses. According to CEO Mary Naylor, VIPdesk hires home-based agents who are highly resourceful and have prior experience in high-end customer service, travel, and/or hospitality.

The company describes its service as "the high-valued gift of time and convenience." *Anything, Anytime, Anywhere* is its descriptive trademark. Services include:

- Dining recommendations and reservations.

- Air, hotel, and auto rental reservations.

- Purchasing event tickets.

- Assistance with special-occasion gifts.

- Scheduling household services.

For example, car owners have access to a VIPdesk concierge by pressing an in-car button or dialing a 24/7 number. They're connected to a VIPdesk concierge who helps them with answers to all types of questions, including finding a hotel that takes dogs while on a road trip, securing restaurant reservations in the nearest city, or finding an activity that would be appropriate for kids at the final destination.

Sometimes the requests from clients aren't as straightforward. For example, a concierge might be asked to locate the handbag carried by a movie star in the latest blockbuster film.

Many agents are employees and, as such, they receive benefits including: insurance (health, disability, and life), paid holidays, and time off, a 401(k) plan, training, and mentoring and rewards programs.

Employees are expected to work at least fifteen to twenty hours per week and earn an average of $17 to $25 per hour, with opportunities to rise into manager and recruiting positions, also all virtual. Positions are competitive and candidates undergo a rigorous review that includes a background check.

Got these?

If you'd like to become a virtual concierge, typical qualifications include:

- Customer service experience with a hospitality orientation.

- An interest in working weekends and holidays.

- Computer experience and technology requirements detailed on the employer's website.

- A quiet, dedicated home office with door locks to ensure data security.

- Outstanding communication skills and phone manner.

- Detail orientation and the ability to problem-solve and multi-task.

Contact these:

Among companies that hire virtual concierges are VIPdesk.com and CharmCityConcierge.com.

Virtual Customer Service Agent

Remote customer service is growing by leaps and bounds. Working as a home-based customer service agent means answering what's known as inbound customer calls for companies like J. Crew, 1-800-Flowers, Virgin Atlantic Airlines, Walgreens, and many others that are outsourcing customer service to companies that hire U.S.-based virtual agents.

The businesses tell us they get higher quality work from at-home agents than they do from those corralled in call centers where turnover is high and working conditions can be unpleasant. Also, for many companies that care deeply about their brand image, U.S.-based agents are often preferable to off-shore hires.

If you're a people person who enjoys telephone contact and

can easily establish rapport, this can be a great niche. Expect to earn an average of $8 to $15 an hour depending on your level of experience, call volume, and the number of accounts you're assigned.

Most companies will expect a minimum of twenty hours per week, although some virtual agents work as much as forty to sixty hours, schedule and workload permitting. There are currently about 100,000 cyber agents out there with numbers on the rise. Research conducted by the market intelligence firm IDC reveals that the IT consolidation market is expected to grow 6.5 percent from 2004 to 2009, from $18.1 billion to $24.7 billion, outpacing growth of the overall IT market.

This is ideal work for those with "piecemeal" schedules who

Happy at Home

"My life was in a rut. Get up, drive to work, and drive home. Day after day, I followed the same routine. Then, after unexpected company layoffs, I suddenly found myself without a job. I began researching new opportunities and stumbled upon work-at-home options. But I wondered, was working from home a legitimate job for a corporate professional? I wanted a position that would recognize and reward my strong work ethic and provide a career path. However, the thought of eating lunches at my kitchen table, walking down the hall to work, and having free time to tend my garden was too tempting to ignore. Luckily, a home-based customer service agent position with Alpine Access gave me the best of both worlds.

"Working for Alpine Access from home has added a new dimension to my life. I have a job I love along with the flexibility I crave. Initially, I handled customer service calls part-time. After numerous promotions, I am now the company/agent liaison. Home-based positions aren't for everyone. You must work hard and do what you say you'll do. But, the rewards are tremendous. Now I schedule my work around my life, not the other way around. Remember, you don't have to drive to an office to be professional and valued."

—Martha Libby, Colorado

may not be able to devote long stretches of the day without inter-ruptions. Set your own hours and meet family needs as long as you get the job done.

If you're bilingual in Spanish and English, you may have even more to bring to a customer-service operation. Businesses of all kinds are reaching out to the huge and potentially lucrative Hispanic market and that means offering customer service in Spanish as well as in English, among other languages. For 87 percent of the U.S. Hispanic population, Spanish is the preferred language at home, according to the Direct Marketing Association. That translates to lots of opportunity.

Shoot for the top.
AlpineAccess.com is a Denver-based company that's been in the at-home customer service business since 1998. Today, the company employs 7,500 work-at-home customer service agents around the country. Alpine's clients include J. Crew, 1-800-Flowers, Office Depot, and ExpressJet, among others. The service is also used by some of the country's largest financial institutions. In this capacity, you'll process catalog orders, answer customer service questions, and even up-sell callers. A customer may want to order one item, but once you're prompted to recite the specials of the day, that order may double in size. When it does, you'll make extra money.

Alpine Access hires employees, not contractors. That means its personnel have access to health benefits and a matching 401(k) plan. Employees do not have to incorporate and do not have to pay their own taxes. Also, employees may work for just one client (for example, J. Crew) rather than several. Agents self-schedule, choosing their preferred hours and can work as few as twenty hours per week.

Starting rates range from $9 to $14 an hour depending on the account. Agents are paid for every hour they're scheduled to work not on how many calls they take. The company says it's receiving about 200,000 online applications per year and will hire about 3,000 of these as virtual customer service agents. That's a competitive job pool.

Got these?

Is a career as a cyber customer service agent for you? Here are some of the things you'll need, although specifics differ by company:

- An up-to-date computer, high-speed Internet access, and a landline.

- A quiet place to work without interruption or background noise.

- A pleasant phone voice and manner.

- An affinity for problem-solving.

- An unflappable disposition and an ability to stay cool, even when customers become dissatisfied or annoyed.

- Prior sales or customer service experience.

- Bilingual skills, insurance licenses, and technical skills are among the specialized in-demand needs.

Contact these:

These companies are among reputable firms for virtual customer service agents. Read through their websites thoroughly before submitting any information. The more you know about them, the better candidate you'll be. Research AlpineAccess.com, LiveOps.com, WorkingSolutions.com, Arise.com, and West.com.

Virtual Eldercare Agent

With baby boomers reaching retirement age in record numbers, the senior housing market is red hot. So too is an at-home work category known as eldercare agent. These are trained specialists who help clients identify appropriate options. Typically, the service is free to clients, but a commission is paid to the agency by the placement organization.

It's an ideal job for people with backgrounds in sales, health care, real estate, senior day care, and other related fields. Candidates must be creative problem-solvers able to understand and empathize with a variety of potentially complex circumstances.

Virtual eldercare is virtually everywhere.
A Place for Mom (APlaceForMom.com) is the largest referral service of its kind in the country (and growing fast) with more than 290 eldercare agents on staff. The firm assists seniors and their adult children to match up individual preferences and needs with available options. These can range from home care to assisted living, independent living and skilled nursing, as well as Alzheimer's and dementia care.

The business works with over 13,000 senior care providers nationwide. The company hires individuals as employees and offers benefits plus reimbursement for expenses.

The ideal candidate is a self-motivated, detail-oriented, entrepreneurial individual with sales experience. Candidates should understand the elder-housing industry and be passionate about working with families. New "Mom" hires must complete a three-day training session, known as "Mom University" at their Seattle headquarters. This is followed by a three-month training program during which new hires receive hands-on support and are mentored by coaching staff.

The company pays for the training and covers the expenses of an annual sales meeting. Advisors are employees on straight commission and receive benefits, including 401(k), stock option plans, and healthcare insurance. As for expected earnings, a company spokeswoman tells us the average first-year earning potential is around $40,000 and the future earning potential is unlimited with no cap on commissions.

Got these?
To be a virtual eldercare agent you need:

- An up-to-date computer, high-speed Internet access, and a landline.

- Experience in sales, health care, or other related industries.

- Dedication to details and lots of perseverance.

- Time management and communications skills.

- Compassion, patience, and the ability to cope with potentially emotionally charged scenarios.

- Understanding of seniors' specialized needs in areas such as health care, accommodations, memory issues, medication, and family dynamics.

Contact these:
Among firms that hire virtual eldercare advisors are APlaceforMom .com and Care.com. Search online for local eldercare referral networks in your area that hire home-based agents to service the community.

You Mean I Have to Interview for This?!

Just because you're working from home doesn't mean you get a pass on some of the traditional work requirements, like the interview. If you're applying to become a virtual customer service agent, telemarketer, or virtual assistant it's likely this will happen by phone.

Even though you're not sitting across the desk from an interviewer in your best dark suit and pumps, you still need to prepare if you want to be remembered and hired.

The interviewer for virtual customer service or other home-based jobs is judging your phone and computer skills, as your voice becomes the virtual "face" of the company to its callers. Here's what we recommend during your interview:

Practice. The decision makers tell us one area where people tend to stumble is the voice test in which you're required to read a script. Failing at this can often mean you've lost your chance, so be sure to practice reading the scripts you'll be provided.

Here's an example of a script, courtesy of LiveOps:

> *"As a thank-you for purchasing the Mini Oven today, Widget Company has a very special offer that includes additional accessories for your Mini Oven that you wouldn't want to be without! This accessory package includes two additional nonstick baskets and the nonstick Round Rib basket. We are also including a 240-page cookbook with over 200 mouthwatering recipes for your Mini Oven. This accessory package has a value of $162, but you can have this package today for only $39.95."*

Read into a recording device, then play it back and critique yourself. Now do it again. And again. Try to sound genuine, calm, and concerned—the way you'd like a customer service agent to sound when you call a company with a tricky problem. Avoid that boring, monotonous tone.

Be flexible. When the interviewer or application system asks about your schedule, express a willingness to work at least fifteen hours a week. Don't go into a long spiel about your kids' schedules and when you need to be home to fix supper. Your would-be employer wants to know you're available and easy to work into the schedule. Offering to take less popular shifts (like nights, weekends, and holidays) makes you more attractive to prospective employers. Then, once you've proven yourself, you should be able to get a more desirable schedule. But first, get your foot in the door.

Tout your techno. You'll want to try to impress the company with your skill and comfort level with technology. If you're great on the phone, but weak on the computer, rectify that before the interview process. It may mean taking a computer course online or at a local community college. Virtual work is dependent on computers, so you'll want to be sure your skills are strong.

You better shop around. No matter what type of business you're considering, check out several to see which offer the best fit. Think long-term about which ones offer the most opportunity for solid growth and success. If incorporating or buying a new computer seems daunting, remember—you're investing in you.

ACTION STEPS

What characterizes this job category is that you're meeting a need rather than starting a business that did not previously exist. Depending on the company, you may be hired as an employee or as a contractor.

You may have to incorporate, purchase equipment, or seek training. You may be required to have several years of industry experience or you may be able to close the gap with a training program, possibly one provided by the company.

If this sounds like the at-home scenario you've envisioned, take these action steps to learn more about what's out there and how you can get your foot in the door:

1. *Invest some time on the websites* of the category that's closest to your interests, skills, and experience. Print off relevant material and begin to assemble a binder. Getting organized is a good way to demonstrate (even to yourself) that you're serious. The large, traditional job boards (HotJobs.com, CareerBuilder.com, Monster.com, etc.) are also good resources for ideas and leads.

2. *Make a simple spreadsheet* (or its equivalent—a hand-drawn chart) as a way to gather and compare requirements, responsibilities, and compensation for a particular industry or category with your skill set.

3. *Find someone to talk to* who is doing exactly what you think you want to do. Search via the websites or through your circle of friends to find someone you can call or e-mail. You may also use message boards and online social networks, including Linkedin.com for finding possible contacts. Jot down a list of questions you wish to ask and take notes during the conversation. Don't limit your questions to all things positive. Ask about the problems, challenges, and potential red flags. You should also ask about realistic earning potential. Even though money may be a sensitive subject, don't shy away from it.

4. *Talk to the experts* who seek and use at-home workers. Call a company and set a time to talk to a recruiter. But instead of him or her interviewing you, you ask the questions before deciding if you want to go further with

this company. Ask about a typical day, the challenges of the role, the realistic compensation, and the turnover rate.

5. *If you feel you're fairly sure* this is the category you'd like to pursue, begin to create an action plan for making it happen. Start at the end by setting a date by which you'd like to make the transition. Then list the things you must do each week to reach that goal, such as researching the options, determining whether or not you meet the criteria of the positions (both in terms of your skills and experience, as well as the required technical equipment to perform the function), and talking to people who are already involved in the type of work you're seeking.

■ ■ ■

chapter five

Be Your Own Boss

Do you bake fruit pies so yummy that friends and family constantly urge you to go into business? Do you plan world-class family events? Do the necklaces you create rival those seen at the finest craft fairs? Are new ideas constantly bubbling up, even in the middle of the night? If so, you just might be a business waiting to happen.

Ten Million and You

The marketplace for women entrepreneurs is exploding. The Center for Women's Business Research says the number of privately held firms owned 50 percent or more by women is over 10 million. That's more than 40 percent of all businesses in the country. These companies generate some $2 trillion in annual sales and employ about 13 million people.

A Yahoo survey shows that three quarters of Americans have an entrepreneurial bent. And half eventually want to start their own business. The most common reason? The opportunity to do something they love.

As your own boss, you not only get to provide goods or services you're passionate about. You get to do it on your terms—with risks and rewards that are all your own.

From Inspiration to Perspiration

This chapter will help you envision what it takes to convert a good idea into a solid, home-based small business. Notice we didn't say a solid *gold* business. We're not necessarily talking about million-dollar ideas here, though if you get there we'll be thrilled. We're talking about replacing the income you're making at your current job, or making it worthwhile to rejoin the workforce after years away.

From pricing to press releases, we'll assist you with information and resources. We will also take the fear out of creating a business plan by breaking it down into manageable chunks.

Ready to invest your passion, your time, and some seed money into your very own business? Get out your highlighter and read on. You've always wanted to do this—it's finally time to get started.

Entering the "Entrepreneur Zone"

Before you start making lists and clicking on websites, you'll need to start thinking like an entrepreneur. It's a mindset rooted in the desire for independence and a passionate interest in bringing a product or service to market.

An entrepreneur can be someone who:

- Uses home as a base to start a business.

- Organizes and operates a new venture based on an identified need.

- Takes an innovative approach to meet that need.

- Isn't afraid of some risk in order to reap reward.

- Is open to new ways of thinking and working.

The nonprofit group Women Work describes an entrepreneur with four key traits:

- *Self-discipline*: the ability to work long hours at tasks both pleasant and tedious.

- *Self-determination*: trust in her own judgment and inner wisdom.

- *Self-interest*: the ability to act on her own behalf for the good of the business.

- *Self-reward*: pride in a job well done, independent of others' opinions.

Are you curious? Do you have stick-to-itiveness? Are you a creative competitor who can brush herself off and get back up when the hard knocks come? Are you a stickler for detail with a good head for figures?

You may not have all of these qualities, but chances are good you'll see yourself somewhere in these descriptions. Dig deep—if you believe it's in you, it probably is.

Answer these questions and mentally benchmark how you line up.

How strong is your motivation? As chief cook and bottle washer, it will be up to you to organize your time, come up with assignments, and follow through on details. Some owners burn out quickly from the burden of carrying all the responsibility for the success of their business. Running a company can wear you down, but it can also be exhilarating. Motivation and enthusiasm can help get you through the rough times.

Are you a great planner and organizer? One of the reasons businesses collapse is lack of planning. Thorough planning and organization of your finances, assets, staff, schedules, inventory, and production is essential for success. If you're more a visionary than a doer, you may want to consider a well-chosen partner with complementary skills.

Are you decisive? Every time you turn around (especially in the early stages), there's a critically important decision to make. Even those that aren't life and death come at you fast. An ability to think on your feet and make wise choices that move your business forward is essential.

How's your health? Even if your business requires no lifting heavier than a new ink cartridge, good health is a huge plus for business owners. Your hours will be long and probably irregular. Especially during the early years, you'll be catching meals on the fly and you'll wonder how you ever had time for the gym, let alone a manicure. Good mental and emotional health are advantages no new business owner can afford to be without.

Is your family prepared? You may be taking this leap for family reasons, but starting a business can be hard on your spouse and kids. You're putting in time and money that until now have been invested in the family. And there's something big and different competing for your attention. You may have to get used to a lower standard of living, at least until your enterprise turns a profit. Make sure everybody knows what to expect and keep the communication channels wide open.

Do you play well with others? Yes, it's your business. But owners must establish successful working relationships with lots of people, including vendors, customers, employees, bankers, lawyers, and accountants. Doing it from home can be extra challenging—having an employee in close proximity for eight or more hours a day can be daunting for both of you.

Minding *Your* Business

Some people have always known what business they'd go into if they could. We know one woman who is a self-taught lamp-maker. She makes them out of everything from cigar boxes to painted pottery and discarded pieces of wood. When the opportunity came to do her own thing, there was no question. Now she's got a successful home-based business.

Others need help finding their niche. Turning an idea, skill, or hobby into a money-making proposition is a matter of knowing the questions to ask, following wise counsel, and ultimately going with your gut.

If you're not completely sure what kind of business you'd like to start, ask yourself these questions:

- Do I want to offer a product or a service?

- If it's a product, what do I know how to make?

- If it's a service, what is my expertise and how will I set it apart from other similar offerings?

- How interested are others in what I have to sell?

- How much money do I have to invest in this dream?

- How much money must I earn to make the effort worthwhile?

Happy at Home

"I began my career as a business owner when I made the decision to leave my full-time teaching position to stay home with my daughter. As a former Spanish teacher with a bilingual husband, the choice to raise our children in a bilingual household was very easy. The word quickly spread in our neighborhood that my toddler was bilingual, and we received requests to host "Spanish playgroups." I began to brainstorm ways I could make money from home and incorporate my passion for teaching. The Bilingual Fun Company was born.

"I started offering parent/child Spanish classes out of my living room. Soon the interest was so overwhelming that I began renting classroom space in a local church. I have a master's degree in bilingual education and two small children who are being raised to speak both English and Spanish, thus my combined experience, knowledge, and everyday life made my business idea a natural choice. My classes became very popular within our community, as we offer classes to children as young as eighteen months through age ten.

"Additionally, my husband and I worked together with a production company to produce a Spanish for Children DVD series. I have been enjoying growth and online sales as we are increasing our marketing to include online, local, and national advertising.

"Armed with my skills and desire to teach Spanish, I have found a wonderful balance between making an income and being at home with my children. For me, creativity, networking, prioritizing, and overall organization have been integral in the success of my home-based business."

—Jennifer Manriquez, Michigan

- Do I have affordable help with the kids and maybe even the house during the start-up period?

- Who can I connect with to learn what it's like to run a similar business?

Think about your daily life: What are you doing when you feel the happiest and most productive? When does time fly by because you're so engrossed in what you're doing? What do the people who know you best praise you for? The answers will help you focus.

Happy at Home

"In 2005, as two old college friends we decided to start our own at-home business. We wanted to remain stay-at-home moms but also wanted to make money selling something we produced just for ourselves. We had different career backgrounds but found common ground in what we were both currently immersed in: motherhood.

"Once we decided to sell cotton apparel that was embroidered with irreverent expressions geared toward moms, we made some prototypes. We wore tees with sayings like "Whine? No. Wine? Yes." around town to gauge the response. It was amazing! Strangers would laugh at the lines on our shirts and ask where we purchased them. That gave us the confidence to move on to the next level: selling to stores and creating our own website PlanetMomTShirts.com.

"Having a web business allows us to work from home during all hours of the day or night. We can answer questions from retailers or customers via e-mail throughout the day. We can fulfill orders in a timely fashion, and make sure our stamp of approval is given to each piece of apparel that we ship. The flexibility of a Web-based business means we can still meet our families' needs. It's the best of both worlds."

—Elise Nappi and Eileen Schneidman, Connecticut

Sky's the Limit

Consider some idea starters. They represent just the tip of the iceberg; the sky is truly the limit when it comes to starting your own shop. As you take into account the kind of business that might work for you, remember that a good idea is not necessarily a new idea. You need not reinvent the wheel to achieve success. In fact, in Thomas Stanley's well-researched book *The Millionaire Next Door*, he makes the case that the most prosaic businesses are often the ones that make people the wealthiest, such as collecting garbage, walking dogs, or owning a series of parking garages.

Think about fast-food restaurants, car dealerships, and coffee shops. Multiple establishments of the same type flourish, even when they're clustered together. Competition isn't always a bad thing. That's because there's a market for what they're selling and the quality, service, and pricing are good. So don't worry if the idea isn't unique. One of a kind is not a prerequisite for success.

One way to figure out what type of business to start is by paying attention to things people complain about. When several neighbors mention they hate walking their dogs, they might become your first customers in a dog-walking and pet-sitting business. For the busy professionals who hate to cook, you might make money preparing homemade dinners.

Who needs what you're thinking of offering? Before you start a business, spend time talking to the people who are likely to become your clients. Ask them what they'd be willing to pay for such services.

Psychographics play a big part in starting home-based service businesses. You can focus on lifestyles, attitudes, motivations, and personalities of the people you'd like to target as customers. What makes them tick? What do they value?

The following entrepreneurial enterprises are representative of the kinds of businesses you could get involved in as a home-based business. There is no intention to provide all the details that you would need in order to make an informed decision about any one of the businesses listed. Your personal due diligence is required in order to seriously consider any one of them.

Author, Author. Are you sitting on the next bestseller or big seller? Whether your passion is cooking, gardening, history, or you have a great personal story to tell, writing a book could just be the right business for you. If you're writing nonfiction, then you'll need to know how to write a book proposal, which is a business plan for the book and is necessary for your book to sell to a publisher. If you're writing a work of fiction, then you'll need to write the entire book and have a complete manuscript.

Understand the publishing world; it's a complicated one. Publishers specialize in subject areas. A traditional publisher will purchase the rights to your book and pay you an advance against sales. If you decide to self-publish, there are many companies to take on your project, but do your homework and select wisely.

Ask yourself this: Does the world need another book on your subject? What benefit are you providing and what makes this book a standout? Authorship is a wonderful opportunity to work from home and make your wildest dreams come true. To get started, investigate whether or not the market is flooded with books on your topic. If you've only developed a book idea or a plot or set of characters, but haven't yet written anything, then you need to get motivated. A good way to begin writing is to write a page a day at the very least, and before you know it you'll have completed your book. There's no way to predict if your book will bring you fame or fortune, but the satisfaction from completing it just might be the right match for you. To get informed and educated

about the literary world and becoming an author, check out
Author101.com and read Rick Frishman and Robyn Spizman's book
series on book writing including *Author 101: Bestselling Book Propos-
als—The Insider's Guide to Selling Your Work* and *Author 101: Bestselling
Secrets from Top Agents.*

Bead Jewelry Designer. You can either make your pieces from scratch
or buy beads and other materials from a supplier, as long as you have
tools, training, and creativity.

Consider buying a digital camera if you don't already have one to
upload images of your creations onto a website. Start-up costs should
be fairly low, depending on the quality of your materials. There's money
to be made, depending on how many pieces you create, how aggres-
sively you market them, and the quality of the materials. Learn more
from the National Craft Association (CraftAssoc.com) and sell on
Etsy.com.

Cake Baker. Cake baking on a small scale is relatively low-risk.
You might bake for neighbors, friends, and family members. This is
a business that can be done by anyone—no matter the age. If you
grow in size, however, you will need to look into zoning and licensing
issues.

You might market your cakes through hosting parties. Invite a
bunch of friends, ask them to invite a few of their friends, and design a
party around great food and a fabulous cake. Do the same for kids' parties. Prepare gift bags for everyone to take home. Inside the gift bag,
include a beautiful piece of freshly baked cake in a cardboard box. Tie
the box with ribbon and include a decorative card with information on
your business. Print a link to your website on the card.

Design a website that includes photos of your creations, order information, and a little background information on you. For example, you

might explain how long you have been baking and why you enjoy it. Start-up costs include baking supplies, packaging materials, and marketing or advertising.

Creative Talent. Many people with creative and artistic talents claim to have great difficultly finding opportunities if they're not willing or able to work in a fulltime, in-house position. Today it doesn't have to be that way. A growing number of online destinations provide access to thousands of project-based opportunities related to all forms of marketing—from writing radio ad scripts to directing the creation of a campaign. OpenAd.net, Aquent.com, oDesk.com, and Elance.com are just a few of the sites to explore.

Custom Crafter. Some people say knitting is the new yoga. Capitalize on the trend of customization by selling handmade sweaters and blankets personalized for each customer. Consider focusing on a specialty such as baby gifts or menswear.

For extra money, consider hosting knitting classes through a local craft store, continuing education program, or in your home. Check local merchants or competitors to determine your pricing. For customized orders, you can charge a premium.

Ebook Publisher. Writing and selling an ebook is a potential income stream if you have a topic and website that will attract solid traffic among readers who will pay to download your material.

Etiquette Consultant. This is an exciting business in a booming industry. An outgoing personality is a plus, if not a must. And, of course, your own etiquette must be excellent. Successful consultants often speak before large audiences. Market yourself to all types of businesses—especially corporations, which sometimes hire etiquette consultants to work with new recruits, or even seasoned executives participating in high-level meetings. You might also consider specializing in such areas as business etiquette, communication etiquette, children's etiquette, international etiquette, or wedding etiquette. A bride and groom might take your evening course before their big day. Parents may enroll their tweens in your weekend seminar.

Freelance Writer or Editor. This business is right for you if you enjoy writing, have marketing savvy, and enjoy working on a variety of

Happy at Home

"One particular day in October 2005, I was on an emotional roller-coaster ride. That morning, my just published novel, *Without Grace*, received its first review. As I read it, my throat closed up because the reviewer compared the story to *To Kill a Mockingbird*, giving it a rave assessment. Later that very morning, however, my tears of joy turned to tears of shock: My position was abruptly terminated due to major cutbacks for a company I'd been with for over eleven years.

"Prior to losing my job, a number of people encouraged me to freelance as a writer and do publishing consulting. As tempting as it was, I was too frightened to make the decision until it was forced upon me. Yet, only months earlier I had just bought my first home as a newly divorced woman and couldn't risk losing it. Immediately sending out my résumé would probably have been what most sensible people would have done, but since I had a small nestegg to accommodate me for a short time, I decided to see if I could make it on my own and take some time to promote my novel and acquire some freelance gigs. Now as the years have passed, I'm still working from home doing consulting, writing, and publicity. My decision allowed me to travel in support of my novel and I was able to accept an invitation to participate in a discussion for my novel with a book club in Savannah, Georgia. I was also given the time to write my second book, which I'm now promoting. There is a freedom to working from home, but it takes discipline, resilience, and willingness to work long hours, but more important, it takes passion."
— Carol Hoenig, New York

projects simultaneously. Although the hours are flexible, the deadline pressures are relentless. Generally, you will work contract to contract. The pay is dependent upon the kind of writing you do, the clients you target, and your experience. The most seasoned writers will command excellent compensation, which may range from $30 to $150 an hour or may be project-based.

You will need writing samples to get started. If you don't have clips, contact small publications or the nonprofit business sector. Consider contributing a few stories for free and then search for paying opportunities.

Whether you are brand-new or established, join trade associations to network and learn of potential opportunities. Groups to consider include a local press club, marketing association, an Association for Women in Communications Chapter, and Public Relations Society of America Chapter. Check with WritersMarket.com and WellFedWriter.com for more information on rates and growing your business. Other helpful resources include CraigsList.com, FundsForWriters.com, MediaBistro.com, FreelanceWritingGigs.com, WorldWideFreelance.com, and AbsoluteWrite.com.

Gardener. Are you a perennially good gardener? It seems like every neighborhood has at least one resident with a really green thumb. She advises new arrivals on landscaping selections and is valued for her skills. If this is you, consider charging a fee for your talent. Begin with a respectable rate per hour and adjust it upward as you become more seasoned. You can work with your neighbors on selecting the right trees, bushes, perennials, and annuals, but you can also help them on creating themes to their yards and gardens. Part-time work may be found at a local nursery or the garden center of a Lowe's or the Home Depot. Customers in those stores often look for someone who moonlights to tend to their gardens.

Home Stager. Home staging is a term popular with real estate agents. People who stage homes often work hand-in-hand with real estate agents or brokers to make a home more attractive before it goes on the market. They have a keen eye and can generally make cost-effective changes. They may also work with home-builders to decorate furnished model homes. And they work with individuals—helping to rearrange furniture, choosing new paint colors, using accessories, and otherwise freshening up. You can stage homes without any official training or certifications. Charge an hourly rate based on what the local market can bear.

Home-Based Child-Care Provider. With record numbers of women working outside the home, caring for children can be a solid enterprise. In fact, the National Association of Child Care Resources estimates that seventy-five percent of children under five are in some type of child care.

When they searched for the perfect nanny in *Mary Poppins*, Jane and Michael Banks's requirements included "a cheery disposition, rosy cheeks, no warts, play games, all sorts." The same holds true today. You'll also need a great love for children, patience, and an appropriate home and yard.

Check with your county about licensing and other requirements. Start slowly with a few children of family and friends. Spread the word through your place of worship or neighborhood association. When it comes to services for their kids, parents appreciate personal recommendations. You can also register your services on SitterCity.com, Care .com, and CraigsList.com to have the customers find you.

House Sitter. As a house sitter, you're hired to bring peace of mind to traveling owners and for specific purposes like watering the lawn and garden, feeding the fish, accepting package deliveries, or keeping an eye on the swimming pool. Maybe they are having their house painted and want someone trusted to be present in their absence. You'll want to screen your clients as carefully as they screen you. You wouldn't want to end up staying in a filthy house or discover late into the game that you are really safeguarding the place against an angry ex-spouse.

Begin by marketing your service among an extended network of family and friends. E-mail everyone you know, encouraging recipients to forward your availability to their friends who may be interested in the service. You can also advertise to extended social groups, such as members of your place of worship. Rates vary a great deal depending on your location. Research your competition. By providing extra services that your competitors do not, you can justify charging higher rates.

Image Consultant. This is a great home-based business, especially if you have previously succeeded in the workplace and really know what it takes to get ahead. So if you were successful in the corporate world and left to start a family, this business might be for you. You can be paid thousands of dollars a day to be an image consultant to a large corporation. What you are teaching people is essentially how to play the game. You advise them on the look and mannerisms that connote success. Think *What Not to Wear* and *Queer Eye for the Straight Guy*.

As an image consultant, you help people make a good impression. This may involve makeover consulting, but also etiquette, nonverbal communications like posture and eye contact, and even things like grammar and vocabulary. Corporations may hire you to work with a new supervisor on how to communicate more effectively with employees. Or you may be hired to ready clients for sales presentations and client meetings. Individuals may seek your hourly services if they're seeking a career boost or promotion. Entrepreneurs who have to polish their appearance are likely clients, too. Research local rates to determine your fees. Build a client base by starting close to home. Offer services to five friends in exchange for their photos and testimonials for your website and marketing materials. Google "image consultants" to review the sites of would-be competitors.

Happy at Home

"I am the founder of addSpace to Your Life!—a professional organizing and image consulting agency. I work from a home office and have done so for more than ten years.

"As a travel writer in the '80s, I was on the road forty-two weeks a year. Four years later, I was tired of constantly living out of a suitcase. I wanted to figure out a way to stay in town, work from home, and make a living. I have never worked in an office environment. The small taste of mandatory weekly meetings made me certain that I would not thrive in the day-to-day drudgery of punching a clock or being required to be in an office setting.

"I founded addSpace to Your Life!, a professional organizing and image consulting agency, which I run from my home. My favorite part is the commute past the coffeepot on the way upstairs to the office. The benefits of a home office are enormous. With wireless technology, I can work and write from anywhere in the house. On a beautiful day, I sit outside on the back patio. On lazy days, I stay in bed with coffee and write or call clients from bed until early afternoon (don't tell!). If I am feeling really corporate, I will actually work in my office with a great view of the palms in my backyard.

"The upside is that I can work anytime I wish. I venture outside of my home office to work with clients in their homes, and I like the fact that I don't have to check in or stop by the office after work. Instead, I simply go home and check messages and e-mails. The tax write-offs are also tremendous for home-based businesses. What could be better than writing off part of your mortgage and utilities?

"The major downside of working from home is the temptation to get sidetracked by laundry, dishes, television, or pets. My warning to those considering this lifestyle is this: If you are not self-motivated and self-governing, forget about working from home. Some people need guidelines, time lines, and accountability to stay on track. Those are the people who usually do not fare well working from home. It can also become lonely with minimal social interaction during the day.

"Also, workaholics beware. If you are a workaholic, you cannot easily check out from work because it is always there. I am blessed to be able to check out from work mentally by simply closing my laptop and my office door. As a lifelong entrepreneur, I will probably always have a home-based business. I have no desire to open an outside office. I prefer to handle my extra work with virtual assistants. This provides me the flexibility to do what I wish, when I wish. It is unstructured and this makes my artistic, creative soul very happy!"

—Kathi Burns, California

Interior Decorator. Interior decorating is very much in vogue primarily due to programs like *Trading Spaces* and *While You Were Out*, not to mention Martha Stewart and even Oprah Winfrey. Americans, in general, are now spending an increasing amount of money on learning how to turn their houses into retreats. This is a great profession for anyone with a knack for decorating. If you choose to become a full-fledged interior designer, you will need to meet licensing, certification, and educational requirements. Refer to ASID.org and cidinternational.org for more details. Interior decorators focus largely on the decorating finishes of a home, such as furniture, fabrics, wallpaper, and window treatments.

According to the ASID website, to enjoy this field you have to be creative, imaginative, and artistic. You have to be disciplined, organized, and skilled at business. You must also be resourceful with a very good Rolodex to know where to find and buy an array of stuff—from flea market finds to high-end customized pieces. ASID has a checklist of questions that you can ask yourself to determine if this is the right field for you.

Life Coach. Life coaching is another fairly new and exciting way to earn a living. One of the most successful and high-powered coaches is Cheryl Richardson, who has written several bestsellers including *Take Time for Your Life*. A life coach is different from a financial advisor or a therapist. She figures out where her clients are trying to go with their lives, and helps them get there. Many people have "big ideas" but get caught up in the minutiae of daily living and lose track of their goals. A life coach keeps clients on track and guides them.

To succeed, you need life experience and wisdom. You should have good interviewing skills and be able to see beneath the surface of things. A client may be stressed from trying to grow her business and start a family. As a life coach, you may need to advise her on how to navigate these uncharted waters.

You might consider investing in a website and starting a monthly newsletter with your general advice. Consider modern-day problems that you see a lot of your peers struggling with and talk about ways to handle them. Speak at local events to spread your message. Visit CoachFederation.org/ICF/ for more on this line of work.

Makeup Consultant. Were you a girlie girl who loved playing dress-up as a kid? Now you can get paid for it as an adult, transforming your clients into perfection for special occasions. Makeup consultants do more than apply foundation and mascara. They get involved in clients' most special moments like proms, weddings, awards ceremonies, and auditions. It's especially promising if you live in a city with celebrities, musicians, and politicians who often must appear on camera or before large gatherings. Makeup artists are trained in beauty schools and even by working at a cosmetics counter in a busy department store. To make money, you must be willing to market yourself to individuals, through salons, and among wedding planners, photographers, and other service providers.

Massage Therapist. Massage is more popular than ever, especially with mainstream Western medicine acknowledging its health benefits. You'll need to become certified by taking classes. Once certified, you can work the hours of your choosing, perhaps on a contract basis for a day spa. If you work from home, you will need to spend several hundred dollars on a massage table, oils, and even scents and music. The idea is to create a loyal, repeat clientele by offering an irresistible experience. Visit several day spas, see how they work their magic, and incorporate some of their best practices.

Music Teacher. Voice, piano, or other music lessons can be offered in your own home or by visiting your students at their homes. Adjust your hourly fee based on your location and clientele. You may have some very seasoned students with career ambitions and their families will expect to pay more. In fact, they will judge your credentials by how much you charge. Beginner lessons are usually lower than advanced offerings.

Painter/Hanger/Faux Finisher. Many talented painters, paper hangers, and faux finishers work independently. Choosing colors and applying paint and paper are daunting tasks for many people. Though you're home-based, you're not going to be at home much, so make sure the scheduling will work for you.

Faux finishing is a popular business among moms. The process transforms the look of a home like nothing else, giving a metallic, aged, or textured look to a wall. When just starting out, charge a very competitive fee, by researching the local competition and then adjust it upward as you build your clientele. This is a business where you want to collect referrals. Take photos of finished rooms and create an online portfolio of your work.

Get the word out about your business by networking with contractors and decorators. Make friends with all of the local antique store owners. Ask to speak about your services at local ladies' lunches.

Party Planner. If you love to create special events, are a stickler for details, and a whiz at creativity, consider party planning. Start taking photos of your own events and develop some testimonials from friends you've impressed. Consider developing a specialty in children's parties—they're big business in some cities.

It is important to recognize that adult party planning is a business of extreme creativity. Part of your responsibilities is to manage budgets and oversee minute details that leave a lasting impression. You have to be good at micromanaging since from the second a guest arrives things can change. Satisfied clients and their guests become your greatest word-of-mouth . . . or not! Being on top of your game with adult party planning is crucial. The other detail that is critical is communicating with clients and vendors. If you are not completely clear, something could go wrong. What happens when the band takes a break? Does a CD play in the background so guests can talk? Have you checked the sound system and speakers? Are wireless mikes required so the guests can do a toast? Check every detail. There's no substitution for thoroughness and follow-through in this business, no matter what type of party you are planning.

You will like this business if you are outgoing and enjoy being in charge. Since most parties occur at prime time, you will often have to work weekends and evenings, which is a consideration if you have children. You are as good as your ideas, so get to know your audience and clients and propose ideas that excite them and demonstrate how much your involvement is really worth!

You'll need a Rolodex of vendors, including caterers, facilities, bands and other entertainers, florists, and photographers. The work is fun and creative, but it can be tedious and demanding. Learn more from Robyn's *Make It Memorable: An A to Z Guide to Making Any Event, Gift or Occasion . . . Dazzling.*

Personal Chef. Food businesses are sizzling hot, including personal chefs. There are now nearly 10,000 personal chefs in this country serving almost 100,000 clients, with numbers on the rise. Personal chefs typically charge per meal or per day and usually work in their clients' kitchens. Among the primary market segments for this service are busy dual-career couples, and seniors with special dietary needs. Some valuable information can be found at PersonalChefsNetwork.com.

Personal Shopper. If you're great at pulling outfits together and have loads of patience, personal shopping may be your calling. Some people combine personal shopping with wardrobe consulting—reviewing what's in someone's closet and recommending what to toss, what to put together, and what to add. This is a very low-overhead business. There is money to be made if you have a good eye and an awareness of styles, fashions, and trends. Personal shopping also requires knowing each client's likes and dislikes. You should also keep good records of sizes and favorite colors and brands. It's also essential to have good relationships with the salespeople or owners of boutiques and stores. You'll be expected to know all the secrets to sales and insider bargains before they're made public. In addition to working with career women and society ladies, consider partnering with hotel concierges to help them meet guests' needs. Expand beyond clothing to help with holiday or other purchases as well.

Some personal shoppers charge an hourly fee, while others take a percentage of the overall cost of purchases. Some do both.

Personal Trainer. You exercise like crazy and read a lot about health and fitness. Why not put your passion to work helping others who are less experienced and less motivated?

Personal trainers work directly with clients and associate with gyms or community centers. You typically need certification to work with gyms or health-care partners. Resources include the American Council on Exercise (ACEFitness.org), the National Strength and Conditioning Association (NSCA-lift.org), and the National Council on Strength and Fitness (NCSF.org). You can also check with the gyms in your area on recommendations and requirements for certification and pricing.

Pet Portraits. If you're a competent photographer who loves and understands animals, you may want to consider marrying these skills. Creating pet portraits may not be mainstream, but it's certainly an emerging trend. Because it is relatively new, it will be up to you to suggest to your clients how to enjoy a photo of Fido or Fifi. Pet portraits may be used on holiday cards, framed in a place of honor in the home, or used to invite two- and four-legged friends to a pet birthday party. You may wish to offer a calendar featuring twelve images of the beloved creature.

Once you've got some experience under your belt, check out the possibilities of shooting pets and pet products for nonprofit groups or advertising agencies. Create a "petfolio," even if you have to fill it initially with freebies you do for friends and family.

Pet Sitter. Create a service offering premium care to clients and join the billion-dollar pet industry. Your main competition is other pet sitters so you need to find a way to make your service unique, which is often based on your personality. Your primary obstacle is demonstrating that you are trustworthy, caring, and reliable. After all, clients not only turn over the care of their pets to you, they turn over the keys to the house. Fees vary by location, number of pets, and other circumstances. It's fairly repetitious, however. Take on too many clients and you risk burnout.

Because of potential liability, clients may insist that you be bonded and insured before you start working. Check out policies through Pet Sitters International (PetSit.com) but first gauge the desire of potential clients. Start your business by sending flyers and listing your service in your neighborhood newsletter or newspaper. Join local groups and network. Promote your business by talking to people with pets, spending time where pet owners congregate, joining associations that expose you to pet owners, and providing incentives for your current customers to refer you to other potential clients. You will have the most success growing your business in and around your own neighborhood.

Photography. If you click with pics, a home-based photography business may be the perfect thing to focus on. Figure out what you like to photograph. Possible niches include kids, sporting events, weddings and special events, homes and gardens, or nature. Make sure you understand how copyrights work and how to protect the images you create as well as pricing your services. You'll also want to be realistic about the costs, including cameras and editing/post-production equipment.

If you're just getting started, volunteer to take photos for a community or nonprofit group. Or, if you'd like to break into photojournalism, present some photos to a local newspaper and offer them at no cost, provided that you receive credit in the cutline. A website is an ideal way to present your work, but make sure it looks fantastic. And consider finding a mentor, a working photographer you may shadow and possibly assist as you learn.

Professional Organizer. Professional organizers provide a somewhat trendy service. They do exactly what their title implies: They help people get organized, both at home and at work. A shining example of this profession is Julie Morgenstern (JulieMorgenstern.com).

Earning potential varies depending on what you do. There is no standard fee structure for this industry. You don't want to price yourself out of the market, but you don't want to undercharge either. You may charge by the hour or by the project. Make certain that the expectations and the scope of the job are outlined in an agreement before commencing the job. Market this type of business by word-of-mouth, referrals, and direct mail. To get started, visit the National Association for Professional Organizers (NAPO.net).

Publicist. It seems that there are as many publicists working from home as there are in conventional offices. Communications people need only a phone and a computer, which makes working at home easy. Many women transition to work-at-home arrangements after working for a company, firm, or agency for a number of years and building their contact base. You also need media contacts. This business thrives on marketing savvy and as long as you have that, you can make a go of it as a home-based publicist. Consultants work with people in all types of industries, such as entertainment, retail, health care, and apparel, so choose your area of expertise.

Compensation per job varies from hourly or project fees to monthly retainers. Consider establishing a website with your biography, a portfolio, and a client list, but don't underestimate the amount of time, contacts, and skills required to do this job. Publicists can spend hours, days,

Happy at Home

"Life at a PR Agency is notorious for long hours, early career burnout, and challenging environment for work/life balance. When I founded PerkettPR in 1998, I developed an original approach to successfully contend with heavy competition and a crowded market: I established a virtual PR firm where all of my executives work from dedicated home offices. Our unique virtual culture allows me to focus our finances on hiring and maintaining a staff of all senior-level professionals across the country—as opposed to paying for office space and having to hire more junior-level executives and be limited to geographical recruiting.

"Our model offers clients a stronger team with better results—providing us a unique advantage over competitive firms. It also offers my employees a better opportunity to balance both career and family life, a key ingredient to keeping top-notch talent in the long run. Because of this vision, PerkettPR has flourished over the last decade, cultivating a positive reputation for creative vision and consistently exceeding expectations, as well as attracting and retaining talented PR professionals in Florida, Maine, Massachusetts, Michigan, New Hampshire, and California.

"While I have worked from home for a decade now, I recently discovered some new benefits. My oldest son started kindergarten and, although I have a demanding, high-powered career running a multimillion-dollar business, I cherish the half hour each day that I get to drop him off and pick him up at the bus stop—and it means the world to him that Mommy can be there. These are the moments that make me remember why I started a home-based business in the first place."

—Christine Perkett, Massachusetts

weeks, and weekends, sometimes landing a few meaningful bookings. A great book to read about promoting yourself, standing out in the marketplace, and branding is *Where's Your Wow? 16 Ways To Make Your Competitors Wish They Were You!* (Spizman and Frishman).

Real Estate Agent. Working as a real estate agent is a potentially lucrative home-based business, but also requires a considerable investment. You will need to get a license and generally must take thirty to ninety hours of coursework. Easy telecommunications has meant that an increasing number of agents, including many successful ones, are working from home. Good agents are part salesperson, part detective, and part psychologist. Patience and strong negotiation skills are a must. The downside of this industry is that you are always on call and often must work evenings and weekends. Talk to at least three agents in your area about the current and anticipated market before jumping in.

Sports Enthusiast. If you're a tennis ace, maybe not even a pro, you can offer lessons to all ages. Whatever your sport, market yourself to country clubs and athletic clubs. Advertise individual and group lessons to children and adults. Depending on where you live, this may be a seasonal or year-round business.

Translator. The translation industry is growing and a translation service is a superb business to start at home if you're also willing to market your availability. Whether you live in a large city, the suburbs, or even in rural America, you've probably observed a huge increase in the number of foreign-born, even non-English speaking people in your community. If you are bilingual or highly proficient in a second language, you can probably find work as a translator.

This industry generally attracts entrepreneurs. Of the approximately 3,000 U.S. translation companies, the majority are home-based businesses. They are launched with an investment in basic office equipment—computer, modem, fax machine, a few dictionaries, and a dedicated phone line. You can live anywhere and work as a translator, but you can't expect the work to find you.

This might include working for an employer who needs you to translate at a weekly staff meeting. You might be hired by a local law firm that must ensure that its lawyers and clients are speaking the same language.

There are also various organizations that hire freelance translators. Among them: WeLocalize.com, Telelanguage.com (which offers telephone translation services), SDL.com, The American Translators Association (ATANet.org), and Accurapid.com. You will likely be required to take a written test and sign a nondisclosure agreement if you sign on with one of these. They prefer native speakers.

Tutor. Tutoring can be lucrative—ranging from $30 to $100 an hour in some communities. Students of all ages, including adult learners, are the target. You don't need a license to become a tutor; a college degree with advanced knowledge in a subject area will do. But knowledge alone won't do the trick. You must possess an ability to help others learn and retain information. College entrance exam tutoring is a hot subfield. Some tutors are referred by a teacher, school, or district, which is a great way to build business. Learn more at the National Tutoring Association (NTATutor.org). For more information on home-based online tutors, see Chapter Four.

Track the Trends

While these are just a sampling of options, our goal is to show you the range of seemingly simple to challenging opportunities. Think about these hot trends as you consider the type of business you'd like to launch. Each one of these can be turned into money-making ventures from home:

- **Food.** Coffee, wine, chocolate, healthy meals, and desserts are among the favorites.

- **The environment.** Going green is big business.

- **Science and technology.** Advances here enable services of convenience to sprout regularly.

- **Senior services.** As boomers age, this sandwich generation needs help for itself and its elders.

- **Health.** Good health and fitness are top of mind as we all strive to extend our lifespan.

- **Kids.** From education to cooking classes, parents spend a pretty penny on cool things for kids.

- **Baby boomer career counseling.** From raising kids and managing eldercare demands, to financing retirement, the needs are enormous.

- **Specialty apparel and plus-size products.** Beauty comes in all shapes and sizes and women aren't willing to conform to one standard.

The website SpringWise.com reports more on the findings of some 8,000 trend watchers across the globe and offers interesting insights to potentially explore.

Resources

There is a universe of information and individuals to support your entrepreneurial success.

SCORE

SCORE (score.org) calls itself "Counselors to America's Small Business." This organization is composed of a small army of over 10,000 volunteer executives (both working and retired) representing scores of different industries and performing confidential counseling. They deliver advice and training through nearly 400 chapters nationwide where businesspeople can participate in one-on-one counseling and attend low-cost workshops.

Who Needs a Million?!

Search the Internet using the words "million-dollar idea" and you'll be directed to tens of thousands of sites in a nanosecond. Everybody, it seems, is chasing that illusive dream.

Attractive? Maybe, but not very realistic. According to the Women Presidents' Organization, only about three percent of women-owned businesses realize revenue that exceeds $1 million. (Don't feel bad: Men don't fare much better. Only six percent of their small businesses exceed the $1-million mark.) The Center for Women's Business Research says revenues for more than 70 percent of these companies is under $50,000.

Aim high but don't limit yourself to a definition of success that's followed by six zeroes. Plenty of at-home entrepreneurs who started off with a great idea and a megadose of enthusiasm have made it well beyond that $1-million mark. But picking up $30,000 or $60,000 a year wouldn't be half-bad either!

The smart money is on a sustainable business that doesn't cost your life savings to launch. But once established, it will generate income that makes it worth your while.

More than a million entrepreneurs use the organization's website each month. It's chock-full of free information like:

- How-to articles and templates for business documents
- 24/7 business advice
- Free e-newsletters
- Success stories and best practices

There's also lots to learn about small-business financing, technology, and disaster preparedness, plus special assistance for veterans and minority-owned businesses.

Inspired by smeared peas

SCORE is well-respected in the business world and has helped turn start-ups into stars. Examples include Jelly Belly candy, Vermont Teddy Bear, and Vera Bradley designs.

But thousands of lesser-known companies have benefited from the organization as well. These businesses may never become household names, but they've made it.

One such entrepreneur is Mente Connery, a Florida teacher whose baby daughter did what they all do: She threw peas from her high chair and smeared them in her hair.

Connery fought back! She invented the Clip-Away Feeding Tray, which attaches to the front edge of a high chair and helps prevent spills by holding a bottle, baby food, and utensils safely out of baby's reach. Connery was recommended to SCORE by a patent attorney.

She met with SCORE counselors who advised her on marketing, branding, sales projections, pricing, and profit margins. The product has sold well and, assisted by SCORE, Connery turned a great idea into a great business.

The U.S. Small Business Administration

The Small Business Administration (SBA) is an independent federal agency created in 1953 to assist and protect the interests of small businesses as a way to help the nation's economy. The SBA helps Americans build and grow businesses. Like SCORE, the agency works through an extensive network of field offices and has partnerships with public and private organizations.

You'll find a great deal of solid information on the website, SBA.gov. The section on home-based businesses is especially valuable. The agency operates a series of Small Business Development Centers throughout the U.S. and they provide free counseling and seminars.

Other Resources

We also recommend:

- Entrepreneur (Entrepreneur.com): More than 200,000 pages of how-to content including expert columnists, listings, tools, and services to help start, run, or grow your dream business.

- Startup Nation (StartupNation.com): An informative site addressing basics like business plans, patents, and sales tools. Plus a weekly e-newsletter and online seminars.

- Inc Magazine (Inc.com): Advice, tools, and services on all aspects of running a business, including fading capital and managing personnel.

- Wall Street Journal Start-up Journal (StartUpJournal.com): Content from the *Wall Street Journal* and exclusive articles and resources on every aspect of starting a business.

- Count Me In (CountMeIn.org): A champion for women's economic independence and the first online microlender. It uses a unique credit scoring system to make loans of $500 to $10,000 to women across the country who need to secure that first business loan. The group provides consultation and education.

- My Own Business (MyOwnBusiness.com): Courses designed to help owners of small- and medium-size businesses, ranging from business plans to marketing, licensing, financing, e-commerce, and franchise opportunities.

Nuts and Bolts

Don't be afraid of words like "business plan" and "sales projections." The nuts and bolts of a business, even a very small one, can be demanding but they don't have to be overwhelming. What's more, there's wonderful free information out there to help you through.

In general, beware of scams related to establishing or operating a business. When you read a posting online or in the back of a magazine that boasts, "Send us $200 and we'll send you a new business start-up kit," you should say, "No, thanks." Any person or company that promises big bucks but says you don't need any skills is likely a scam. Similarly, an ad that asks you to send money but doesn't allow you to talk to someone first is one to steer clear of.

The Business Plan

A business plan is an important business tool and there are many ways to write one. While it might seem like another useless document, the truth is quite the opposite. A detailed business plan keeps you on track and communicates (especially to you) the focus of your business, providing a blueprint and a systematic program for all that must be in place before, and after, you open for business.

Although there is no single right way, there are plenty of wrong ways to go about this. The business plan is a framework for your business idea. It is unique to you and your business and takes into account your individual perspective. A business plan is a necessity if you are seeking financial support; lenders typically want to see one before considering your request.

There is no shortage of information about writing a business plan. Government agencies provide free information. Private companies will help you write one. There are numerous books devoted exclusively to the topic. Start with an Internet search to identify the various components that could be included in your plan. Write a little bit a day if the process overwhelms you, but don't delay this important step. You'll also need a sales and marketing plan and a pricing structure.

Developing a business plan forces you to think about every facet of running a business, including those you know less about or don't think you'll like doing as well. The plan does not have to be formal or fancy. Remember, just because you create a business does not mean your customers will come. You have to create success; a plan helps you do that.

There are many templates and sample business plans at the website Bplans.com. Depending on the kind of business you wish to start, familiarize yourself with SBA.gov, the website of the United

States Small Business Administration. As mentioned earlier, the SBA maintains and strengthens the nation's economy by aiding, counseling, assisting, and protecting the interests of small businesses and by helping families and businesses recover from national disasters. You'll find excellent overall business planning advice at SBA.gov.

Elements of a Business Plan

- Description of the business

- Mission statement

- Marketing plan

- Finances and pricing

- Management and operating procedures

Financial Data to Consider

- Loan applications

- Capital equipment and supply list

- Balance sheets

- Break-even analysis

- Profit-and-loss statements

- Three-year summary

- Detail by month, first year

- Detail by quarter, second and third years

- Assumptions upon which projections were based

Legal Matters

It may not be as much fun as creating the product, but depending on the nature of your home-based business you will need to address a variety of legal issues. You may even need some hours with a lawyer and a CPA. Consider the following:

- Decide upon the legal structure of your business.

- Register the name of the business with your state. Most states have a process online for registering names. See Business.gov. MyCorporation.com helps owners and entrepreneurs start, protect, market, and manage their businesses. The site also offers a free trademark search.

- Determine whether your enterprise will require any local business licenses and apply. The Chamber of Commerce in your area may be of assistance with this.

- Obtain a sales tax number from the state if you must charge sales tax.

- Obtain a federal tax ID number if you have employees or are incorporated. Visit IRS.gov or phone the IRS for a free Small Business Tax kit at (800) 829-3676.

If you will need to hire employees, create job descriptions, or determine salary levels and benefits, the Department of Labor site (dol.gov) has useful information.

Get Down to Business Checklist

- Register the name of the business with your state. Most states have a process online for registering names: Business.gov.

- Get business cards and stationery printed. You might also be able to create these on your home computer using simple software available at your local office supply store. At this stage, you are looking for cost-saving measures while preserving a professional image. Consider what information must be on your business card. If you don't want your home address listed, perhaps you'll need to get a post office box address, but keep in mind the amount of time you'll also spend going back and forth to the post office or nearby resource. Think through these details and make sure you create these essential items in the best possible way. The best cards communicate what you do and how to reach you.

- Determine whether your business requires any local business licenses and apply. Obtain a sales tax number from the state if you have to charge sales tax.

- Designate some office space in your home with phone line, computer hookup, and whatever is applicable to your needs.

- Determine how much of your own money you can afford to put into the business. Remember, you might not be generating income for a while so you've got to have your personal finances in order. Don't risk essential money that would normally cover your necessary expenses.

- Consider taking a class or classes so you can understand all the aspects of running a business. There are many free classes offered by a variety of institutions, nonprofit organizations, community centers, and government programs. Free information could save you time and spare you stress.

• You'll find useful links to online programs and tutorials related to business education at OnlineWBC.org.

Financing and Pricing

Getting sufficient capital—whether it's only a few hundred dollars or a couple thousand dollars—is an important factor in starting a new business. It can make or break a venture and it's the source of most of the start-up stress. Even without a strong financial track record and great personal wealth, raising the funds necessary to start up is within reach for many.

In beginning your search for financing, first determine your strategy for obtaining the money to start your business. Begin with these questions:

• How much of your own money can you afford to put into the business? Remember, you might not be generating income for a while so you've got to have your personal finances in order.

• Can you approach family and friends? Would you feel more comfortable asking for a loan, which you'll repay, or an investment in your efforts? If it's a loan, what are the terms of repayment? Is the lender prepared to lose money if the business doesn't take off?

• How about using credit cards or a bank loan? Make sure you've got good credit so you'll qualify for a low interest rate. Always have some credit in reserve to cover unexpected expenses.

Depending on the expected sales volume, open a separate bank account for your business at a customer-friendly bank. The bank may require a copy of your business license before opening the account, so pop in to ask for requirements.

Pricing is tied into your financial structure. What will you charge for your product or service? Women frequently tend to undercharge. Charging too much can scare off potential customers, while charging too little appears to diminish the perceived value. Check out the competition and learn what the market is supporting.

A pricing strategy starts with assigning a value to the materials used, as well as your time. Then, determine what the market can bear through basic research. One entrepreneur we know wanted to offer sewing classes in New Jersey. So she researched other courses in the area and held an informal focus group in her living room over cake and coffee. She asked participants what they would consider paying for classes and combined that with her calculation of the value of her time.

Name that Business

Choosing a memorable and meaningful name for your business is very important. A name does many things. At the very least, it describes your business. It also can suggest the personality you want your business to convey. A name like Corporate Computing Services might appeal to Fortune 500 companies. But a name like Connie Can Compute! suggests a more fun, casual approach that could appeal to a mom-and-pop audience.

A name is a marketing tool; just think of all those businesses named Acme because it was first in an alphabetical listing. Think about the customers you want and select a name that reflects their interests and needs. Make sure the name of your business communicates what you'll do.

You can provide a service or operate a business under your own name, but if you'd like something catchier or more descriptive, say, A+ Tutoring instead of Jane Smith, Tutor, you'll need to search county and state records to make sure the name isn't already taken. Work through your state's Secretary of State or other appropriate office to register your "fictitious, assumed, or doing business as" trade or business name. For clarification on what constitutes a fictitious or doing business as (DBA) name, see Nolo.com. You'll also need to conduct a search before registering a business trademark with the United States Patent and Trademark Office (USPTO.gov).

If you're planning to take your company national, incorporate, or have an Internet presence, your search will need to be more extensive and thorough to make sure it isn't competing with any other company that could challenge you in court. Sites like Check domain.com can help you search and register your domain name for a website. Lawyers and business name search firms can also help. Don't order business cards, stationery, signs, or print materials until after you know your name is registered.

Happy at Home

"In trying to select a name for my T-shirt business, I had always called my son a little stinker. Since I wanted a name to celebrate both of my kids, I came up with StinkyKids.

"Fun, fabulous, and fashionable, StinkyKids is a company dedicated to celebrating the innocent and simple joys of childhood.

"'You little stinker' is an expression that has rolled off the lips of parents for decades. The phrase is affectionate and playful—with a nod to the freewheeling fun of childhood. Visit stinkykids.com."

—Britt Menzies, Georgia (stinkykids.com)

You may wish to search two or three possible names. Then, once you know they're available to you, run an informal focus group with family, friends, colleagues, or potential customers. Review the names and ask their preferences and reasons. Remember, you're going to have to see, hear, and live this name for a long time. Make it good!

Marketing and Promotion

How will you reach your potential customers? You can't just create a website, whip up some flyers or put out a shingle and expect people to come knocking. Consider these options to spread the word about your products and services:

- Cold calling.

- Offer free consultations.

- Speak at local functions about your new business and your area of expertise. (For example, someone who does antique appraisals out of her home might offer to speak about collecting at a local charity event. This provides valuable exposure for her business.)

- Run contests, samplings, and giveaways. (If you're promoting your home-cooking business, bring samples to the annual fair at your kid's school to let busy working parents sample your food.)

- Distribute e-newsletters. (Create an e-newsletter about your expertise, services, and news about your business that you distribute by e-mail to all of your friends and family, asking them to forward it to their lists.)

- Seek referrals from satisfied customers.

- Post flyers at schools, religious institutions, community bulletin boards, and other well-trafficked spots.

- Create a website (this can be done for as little as $10 per month), then attract customers to it by sending out e-flyers to your entire mailing list and encouraging each recipient to tell five other people about your new business. The website 1and1.com walks you through low-cost website development, including selecting a domain name and building your site. You can complete the process in a day if you're patient.

- Write press releases for your local newspaper. Small-town publications are especially eager to fill their pages and will often print what you provide. Also aim for pick-up on blogs that will link back to your website.

- Join business, professional, and social networking groups (in person and online) to spread the word about what you offer.

- Sell your wares on eBay. There's a built-in customer base that numbers in the millions.

- Consider partnering with other complementary small businesses in your area and seek publicity for your affiliation.

- Donate your product or service to charity auctions to gain visibility.

- Invite friends and family to use or consume your product for free. But require them to complete a simple feedback form so you can learn more about how to reach them and convert them to paying customers.

- Offer limited-time, introductory pricing.

Remember that marketing and promotion are not one-time or start-up activities. Coca-Cola, McDonald's, and other top brands never let their name fade from your consciousness. Be sure to back up your claims about what you're selling. You must deliver on what you promise.

Make Money via Your Website

Building a website and making money via online advertising is not just for kids anymore. People of all ages are generating cash without master-level technical skills. They're tapping into the Google AdSense system run by the global search giant.

Contextual or content-sensitive online advertising is on the rise. In 2006, Google says it shelled out $3.1 billion to AdSense publishers, up from $1.2 billion in 2004. Contextual means the ads have a relevance to the content of the website on which it appears, thereby increasing the chance of visitors clicking on those ads. When visitors click, the website's owner gets paid.

There are four steps to get started.

Build a website. If you know how to send e-mails, navigate AOL, or shop on eBay, then you're likely quite capable of building your very own website. Select a topic that you're truly passionate about since you'll be living and breathing it for quite some time.

Google offers two free tools that have their advertising program built in—Blogger.com and Pages.Google.com—but you're by no means limited to using their tools. Sites such as Microsoft's Smallbusiness.officelive .com, Yahoo Publisher, GoDaddy.com, and Apple's iWeb all have programs that allow users to build their own sites. If you already have a website, you're ready to go.

Register for Google ads. Most of us have no interest or expertise in going out and selling ads to appear on our websites. But that doesn't mean you can't snag even a sliver of the online advertising bucks.

Register your site with Google's AdSense program (Google.com/AdSense), which works with hundreds of thousands of websites and hundreds of thousands of online advertisers. Signing up is free, with no cost and no obligation. The system matches the advertiser's target audience with the content of the relevant websites.

For example, you might create a website about everything there is to know and love about beagles. When you register for Google's AdSense, the ads appearing on your site will relate to that subject—ranging from dog food and breeders to pet accessories, insurance, and maybe even Halloween costumes for pets. You're not going to find ads for computers or cars; all of the ads will be relevant to your overall content. You will earn money—from pennies to dollars—every time someone clicks on those ads.

To host the ads, Google provides site owners with simple code to embed on various pages of their websites. The location of those ads is determined and controlled by you. Google's system replaces ads daily, thereby maximizing your chances of capturing new clicks often.

Even though Google's network is the largest of its kind, there are also other ad sites you can explore before deciding who to register with. Among them: Yahoo (Publisher.Yahoo.com), Adbrite (Adbrite.com), and Text Link Ads (Text-Link-Ads.com).

Add new content regularly. Since you only make money if visitors to your site click on the ads, there are two things you can do to build an audience. One of those tasks is to add fresh unique content often. Depending on your financial goals, you might have to commit to working on your site every day by adding new content. The more pages of content you have, the more ads you can host, and the more potential you have to make money. A site with five pages won't make nearly as much money as a site with fifty or 500 pages of relevant content.

A website about beagles might feature well-researched content on breeding, training, and grooming. It may also include a section about what your puppy is up to, along with tips and tricks you've used to train him. You might post questions on your site soliciting advice from your readers to help you to get him to stop biting your kids. You might also compile a frequently updated list of famous people who have owned beagles. The possibilities are endless for refreshing the content.

If you're just looking to make a nominal amount of money, then you can add new content less frequently. Adding more content—and not just junk, but valuable stuff that someone who cares about your subject matter would enjoy reading—will increase the number of people you'll ultimately be able to attract. And the more traffic you have, the more likely it is for some of those visitors to click on the ads.

Promote your website often. It's not nearly as simple as "Build it and they will come." That's true with any business or resource. To make money, you must have a solid product and you must hustle to let an audience know it exists.

Some companies spend big bucks promoting their websites, but there are many free things anyone can do, especially if you're starting out with no budget.

- **Contact friends and family.** Send smart, engaging e-mails asking them to visit your site and to refer it to their circle of friends. This helps to build a word-of-mouth following.

- **Submit your site to all of the search engines** so your content will be indexed.

- **Focus on reciprocal links.** I might ask beagle breeders and dog walkers to link to my website and I'll provide links to their sites.

Happy at Home

"I originally developed an interest in honeybees some years ago when I tried to exterminate a honeybee colony that was building a beehive in my backyard. It took a while to kill them, but their tenacity to hang on to life caught my attention. Subsequently, I developed a serious interest in honeybees and beekeeping.

"About three years before I retired from working, in 1996, I started my first two beehives. After retirement, I became active in our local County Beekeeping Association. During this time, I also developed a serious interest in computers and the Internet. I subscribed to some newsletters about how to create and maintain a website. This combination led to the creation of my website, with the goal of educating the public about the benefits of honeybees, as well as an attempt to create an interest in beekeeping as a lifetime hobby.

"Over time, I improved my website creation skills and continued to learn all I could about how to drive more traffic to the site. Now my site gets traffic from practically every country on the planet. Naturally, the bulk of it comes from the major English-speaking countries: the U.S., Canada, the U.K., and Australia. Even so, I have most likely maximized my potential daily traffic. Let's face it: Honeybees and beekeeping occupies a pretty small niche on the Internet.

"I became interested in seeing how I could earn some money through my site, if only to have it pay for itself. I am one of the original 300 to take advantage of Amazon.com's Affiliate Program. As an Affiliate, I insert coded links on my website for visitors to purchase products from Amazon, for which I receive a small commission.

"I also discovered that I could apply to Google to have Google Ads on my website. I went to their AdSense site and read every detail on how to set up these ads and how to optimize them to generate the maximum income. My first month's earnings came to $26.56, and I was thrilled. My wife jestingly said, 'You always wanted to make money doing nothing.' My earnings continued to increase and some months have exceeded $300. It's perfect for the little extras."

—Al Needham, Massachusetts

- **Develop a PR campaign.** Pitch yourself as an expert to the local media and be sure your website is included if you're quoted.

- **Give speeches** in your community on your topic of expertise and promote your site in the process.

In addition to numerous books and websites devoted to helping you monetize your website, Google has an extensive help center with step-by-step instructions (Google.com/AdSense/Support/) as well as the AdSense blog and newsletter that offer lots of tips (AdSense.Blogspot.com/). Google also holds regular webinars for its AdSense publishers. Google won't do the work for you, but a support team will respond to your inquiries within twenty-four hours.

Happy at Home

"In early 2000, I wanted to share my knowledge about cruise travel on the Internet. At that time, there was very little reliable independent and unbiased cruise travel information available online.

"I began with FrontPage, an easy-to-use program that helps create web pages, and researched how best to design a website. To add images, I learned to use Photoshop. From a small beginning with a few pages hosted by my ISP, I registered my domain name and found a hosting service. I formally launched CruiseDiva.com in 2001. My goal was, and is, to help readers make appropriate choices in order to meet their cruise travel expectations.

"Search engines and fresh content are key to my traffic. Readers return to my site to find out what's new. Word-of-mouth is also important and I'm gratified that readers share my website with their friends.

"While I had a few retail affiliate programs associated with CruiseDiva .com, the introduction of Google AdSense was a turning point. AdSense has provided a dependable revenue stream and my website became a profitable venture. I didn't know how to go about getting advertisers on my own and AdSense does it all."

—Linda Coffman, Georgia

ACTION STEPS

Entrepreneurship is alive and well and there's no reason you can't get in on the action. Just keep in mind that growing your own business is a big undertaking. You'll have to work extremely hard to overcome the obstacles, whether it's finding capital, getting a product manufactured, pricing your service, or getting the domain name you want. But the rewards can be great—especially for people who have always dreamed of something that's all their own.

Take these action steps to get closer to becoming your own boss:

1. *Identify three entrepreneurs who have made it* and find a way to reach them by phone, e-mail, through a contact, etc. Develop a list of three to five questions you'd like them to answer.

2. *Create a spreadsheet* that lists the pros and cons of your offering. Think critically about your product or service and don't be afraid to get the views of others you trust.

3. *Develop a financial fact sheet based on answers to these questions.* For example: How much money do you have to invest? How long can you wait to turn a profit? How much will you need to make per month to make it viable?

4. *Sit down with ten people who know your product or service.* Learn what they love about it, what they think could be improved, what will make it sell better, and how much they think it's worth.

5. *Consider a brief stint working for someone else* or shadowing someone in a similar business, even for a few days.

6. *Write your business plan and go through the* business checklist on page 129.

chapter six

■ ■ ■

Succeed in Direct Sales

While everyone's heard of Avon ladies and Tupperware queens, most people are surprised to learn that more than 15 million Americans are involved in direct sales, according to the 2006 statistics issued by the Direct Selling Association. That's an increase of more than one million people from the year before.

While you may dream of earning the keys to a pink Cadillac to celebrate your sales success, direct selling is by no means a get-rich-quick opportunity. In fact, the median income is only about $2,500 annually, which means half of the sellers are making more, while the other half are bringing in less.

Some sellers see it as an ideal way to supplement their households' primary incomes, but a good 20 percent are actually generating more than $20,000 annually and have turned to direct selling as a full-time career.

How It Works

Direct selling is person-to-person sales of consumer products or services taking place outside of a traditional retail location. Direct sellers are independent consultants, not employees. Products are sold primarily through parties, hosted in private homes where you gather a bunch of your friends or you get people you know to invite their friends. One-on-one selling is also an option.

Most direct-selling companies make it easy for you to sell their products: Every seller gets a web page on the company's website from which to take and process orders, so when your customers want to order or reorder, they can do it online. Each time you make a sale, you earn a commission. And if you recruit people to become sellers, you'll make a small commission on their sales, too.

Among the most popular reasons women choose direct selling:

- Work part-time or full-time—you choose when and how much you want to work.

- Set your own financial goals and determine yourself how to reach them. For some women, this means earning a couple hundred dollars per month, and for others it means earning a thousand or more.

- Earn in proportion to your own efforts. In most businesses, the level of success you can achieve is directly related to the time and effort you're willing and able to contribute.

- Receive training and support from an established community.

- Network and socialize with old friends and make new ones, too.

- Anyone is eligible. With most direct sales opportunities, there are no required levels of education, experience, geography, or even physical condition. Women of all ages and from all backgrounds are succeeding in direct sales every day. More than 70 percent of all direct sellers are women.

Is It Right for Me?

The average seller spends less than ten hours a week focused on his or her business. Steer clear of any promise of big bucks or fast cash with minimal effort—that doesn't exist in direct sales. Determine in advance how much time you're willing and able to put in since the rewards are a direct result of the effort expended.

Consider Personality

If you're quite shy, unwilling or unable to hustle, then any form of sales, especially direct sales, probably isn't right for you. Unlike working in a retail store, where customers walk in, with direct sales you're on your own. It's up to you to find those customers. A driven, friendly person who wouldn't be shy about asking her friends to refer her to potential customers, and who isn't shy about chatting up strangers, is a great fit.

If entertaining is your least favorite thing, rethink direct sales. You'll have to do a whole lot of entertaining to generate new customers. You'll also have to ask friends and friends of those friends to host events for you. The company you opt to sign up with will provide details on how to plan and execute your events. They may also offer bonuses for the hostess to help you land a date.

The most successful direct sellers are those people with outgoing personalities who are motivated and driven each day to focus on their businesses. They're thick-skinned—easily able to bounce back from rejection. They aren't offended when someone declines the opportunity to make a purchase.

What to Sell?

Pick a service or product line that you are passionate about. If you can't see yourself using the products or services and giving them as gifts, stay away. You'll likely get bored quickly, which means little chance in successful sales.

Some people prefer to go with a big name, such as Avon or Mary Kay, simply because everyone knows it, which can be comforting with sales. Others prefer to go with a name you've probably never heard of because that too can be instrumental in generating

Happy at Home

"I am a mother myself so I understand that the amount of effort put into a home-based direct sales business cannot always be consistent. Because of this, BabyCrazy does not have any sales quotas or inventory purchase requirements for our sales reps. I have also found that many people are excited to find a newer company like ours that has huge growth potential.

"BabyCrazy offers women the opportunity to be successful without asking them to choose business or family. Women are encouraged to include their children in their business and fit their BabyCrazy activities into their current lifestyle. My job is to educate them on how to write and use a business plan so they learn that setting goals and monitoring progress allows them to build a rewarding home business.

"Another nice thing about BabyCrazy is the fact that age is not a factor when it comes to starting a business. Even grandparents can start their own business easily, regardless of their previous experiences. Because they are so trusted, grandmothers make a great resource for customers who are purchasing baby items."

—Jen Rivaldo, Georgia

sales. Only you can decide what's right for you and your potential customer base. Among those brands to consider that aren't yet household names:

BabyCrazy (BabyCrazy.com) focuses on baby products from diaper bags to safari play sets. Various starter kits range from $99 to $259, and the company is favored by moms and grandmothers who enjoy buying the best for their kids. If you don't like kids or you're never around people with kids, then this isn't the right match for you.

Private Quarters (MyPrivateQuarters.com) has a wide range of high-end bath and bedding, including a top-selling deluxe queen feather bed. The starter kit is about $199 and has led to success for sellers who value good quality home products and limited competition in this category among other direct-selling companies. If you don't mind sleeping on decade-old ratty sheets with stains and tears, then perhaps you'd want to steer clear of this opportunity.

Shaklee (Shaklee.com) offers nutritional supplements, personal-care products, and home-cleaning products. The starter kit is often promoted as low as $39.95. This company has a very cause-oriented distributor force that cares deeply about the environment. There are also plenty of folks who think global warming is nonsense and they'd rather use bleach as their cleaner of choice. If that's you, this isn't a good fit.

Shure Pets (ShurePets.com) carries products for pets and pet lovers with a starter kit for about $99. With prices ranging from $5 to $100, this site is ideal for animal lovers and people with a passion for pets. Keep away if you're allergic to animals and cringe when other people talk about their furry friends.

Tastefully Simple (TastefullySimple.com) sells gourmet food products, the most popular of which is its bountiful beer bread for $4.99. While all products retail for under $10, the starter kit is about $170. The successful sellers love to entertain, socialize, and, of course, eat. Grumpy introverts, wallflowers, and house hermits need not apply!

The Direct Selling Association (DSA.org) offers a list of more than 200 companies in a wide variety of categories with links to their websites. This industry association is also an ideal resource on the industry. Another valuable resource is the Direct Selling Women's Alliance (DSWA.org).

In many cases, the start-up costs provide you with initial materials, supplies, and training manuals. It is not merely a fee to join. Visit the individual websites to get up-to-date information. This is by no means a definitive list of possibilities. We just want to get you thinking and demonstrate how vast this industry really is.

- **Angela Moore** (AngelaMoore.com) Colorful fashions and accessories for women.

- **Arbonne** (Arbonne.com) This company specializes in skin-care products.

- **Avon** (Avon.com) Founded in 1886 as the California Perfume Company, the company officially took on the name Avon in 1937. In 1997, Avon's sales topped $5 billion, with over 2.6 million independent representatives. Avon has built one of the leading distribution chains.

- **Barefoot Parties** (BarefootParties.com) Lisa Hammond, the Founder and CEO of Femail Creations, a mail-order catalog filled with gifts and products to inspire women, created Barefoot

Parties, which offers unique and heartfelt merchandise in a relaxing, exciting party format.

- **Bead Retreat** (BeadRetreat.com) Two women with a love of beading created this business after finding the jewelry selections in stores to be at times limiting.

- **BeautiControl** (BeautiControl.com) Brings the spa experience home by selling beauty products and makeup.

- **Carlisle Collection** (CarlisleCollection.com) This collection specializes in high-end fashion design.

- **Cookie Lee** (CookieLee.com) Started in 1992, inspired by contemporary designs and classic jewelry basics, the line offers a range of affordable fashion accessories.

- **Creative Memories** (CreativeMemories.com) Creative Memories is based on preserving family stories in keepsake albums.

- **Discovery Toys** (DiscoveryToysInc.com) The company offers books, toys, and personal-care products for kids.

- **Essential Bodywear** (EssentialBodyWear.com) Bodywear, undergarments, shape-wear, and loungewear are sold using measurements and fittings in comfortable, home settings.

- **Ethnic Expressions** (EthnicExpressions.com) African-American art and sculpture for the home.

- **Gold Canyon** (GoldCanyon.com) Scented candles and fine fragrances and accessories for the home.

- **Home and Garden Party** (HomeandGardenParty.com) Products include stoneware pottery, candles, lamps, flowers, and bakeware for home and garden.

- **Jordan Essentials** (JordanEssentials.com) Bath and beauty products for adults, teens, and children.

- **Mary Kay** (MaryKay.com) One of the leaders and innovators in makeup and skin-care products.

- **Our Own Image** (OurOwnImage.com) African-American party supplies, gift bags, journals, and home accessories.

- **Party Lite** (PartyLite.com) Decorative candles and fragrances for the home.

- **Princess House** (PrincessHouse.com) Functional cooking, entertaining, and dining products for everyday and special occasions.

- **Quiet Places** (QuietPlacesForYou.com) Candles, pillows, mugs, books, personal care, and more.

- **SeneGence** (Senegence.com) Makeup and beauty products.

- **Signature Homestyles** (SignatureHomeStyles.com) Ideas for everyday living, with premier home products ranging from picture frames to popcorn bowls.

- **Silpada Designs** (Silpada.com) Sterling silver jewelry.

- **Southern Living** (SouthernLivingAtHome.com) Home products and décor including books, magazines, pottery, glassware, accents, and wrought-iron products.

- **Stampin' Up!** (StampinUp.com) Decorative stamp sets and accessories for home décor, greeting cards, craft projects, and scrapbooking.

- **The Happy Gardener** (TheHappyGardener.info) Gardening supplies, container gardening supplies, tools, imported bulbs, birdhouses, and organic fertilizer.

- **The Longaberger Co.** (Longaberger.com) A leading maker of handcrafted baskets.

- **The Pampered Chef** (PamperedChef.com) Professional-quality cooking equipment.

- **The Traveling Vineyard** (TheTravelingVineyard.com) Wine, plus tasting glasses, corkscrews, wine charms, and assorted accessories.

- **Tupperware Corporation** (Tupperware.com) Kitchen products from one of the original direct-selling giants.

- **Worth Collection** (WorthNY.com) Custom-designed, ready-to-wear clothing.

The Challenges

Many people find that they quickly exhaust their social network. Friends may be happy to buy from you once. But unless your products are really serving a need for them, you will probably have exhausted their goodwill after one party. For this reason, there will be a push at the end of the party to have a couple of guests sign on to host their own parties. Be careful with this. This push takes a lot of guests by surprise. Be sensitive to their needs and level of commitment.

Also beware of pyramid schemes. They are often characterized by a requirement that you pay a hefty fee upfront. A legitimate company won't ask you to pay more than the cost of a sales kit. Beware of companies that want you to buy lots of products, no products, or won't buy back your inventory. If you feel confused, pressured, or in over your head, stay away. This is more than good business sense. Pyramid schemes are illegal.

Homework Required

The earning potential in direct sales is right up there, but you'll need to conduct careful research to select the opportunity that best suits you and your potential customer base. We've provided you with a list of some reputable companies, but it's just a jumping off point as you determine the companies that are the best match for you.

We do not endorse these direct sales opportunities or recommend one of them over another. Please promise us you'll do plenty of homework before investing in them. An opportunity for success for one person is a disaster in waiting for another. It is our goal to make you aware of the number and variety of direct sales opportunities available. The responsibility for choosing this form of home-based business over another depends on your personality, your personal

---

Home Helper: Avoid the Red Flags

Researcher and writer Kim Klaver has developed an expertise warning about the potential pitfalls of direct selling. Before diving into any opportunity, consider two red flags that Klaver has seen time and again.

Warns Klaver: "They say, 'It's easy. It's like recommending a restaurant or movie to a friend, only you get paid for it.' Recommending is easy—we do it every day. But when's the last time you charged a friend for the thing you recommended? That's the hard part. Get training and practice in approaches that don't make friends feel used or abused."

Here's another common, and sometimes misleading refrain, according to Klaver, "'It's not selling; it's sharing.' Direct sellers/network marketers usually sell stuff they're passionate about; that part is like sharing. But, unlike sharing a dessert with a friend, you have to make the sale to earn the money. Good news: Avant-garde sales techniques are turning away from manipulation and hype. Instead, they draw on women's natural tendencies to sell with authenticity, trust, and a good story." To learn more visit KimKlaver Blogs.com.

preferences, the comfort level you have with a financial commitment, and the long-term viability of your business opportunity.

Finally, remember that direct sales is an opportunity, not a guarantee for success. Plan for the long haul. Most of your friends will buy a piece of costume jewelry or a glass pitcher from you once. But you will find RSVPs dropping to zero for your next party unless you are bringing something of real value to their lives.

Costs and Fine Print

Make sure you're being asked to pay a reasonable fee, which should cover product samples, training materials—which often include manuals, videos, access to seminars, and more—plus catalogs and order forms. The median fee for a starter kit is $70, and the retail value of the products often exceeds what you're paying for. Don't be sucked into opportunities that call themselves "direct sales" but require you to pay a fee solely for the privilege of becoming a seller. To pay a fee, you should be getting something tangible in return.

You should also be sure that you're selling directly to the consumer. For example, if you're selling food products, make sure that it is food that will go right into the buyer's mouth. There is no shortage of scams that require you to stock up on inventory and with a false promise of teaching you how to unload it to various distributors. That's not direct sales.

Check the Buyback Policy

If you're not satisfied or you discover this isn't right for you, will the company buy back the starter kit? The Direct Selling Association Code of Ethics requires its member companies to buy back the kit and any product for at least 90 percent of what you paid for it within one year of purchase. If the company isn't a member of the DSA, ask directly what the policy is before you make any purchases.

Specifically, the DSA policy states that companies shall "repurchase on reasonable commercial terms currently marketable inventory, in the possession of that salesperson and purchased by that salesperson for resale prior to the date of termination of the salesperson's business relationship with the company or its independent salespeople. For purposes of this Code, 'reasonable commercial terms' shall include the repurchase of marketable inventory within twelve (12) months from the salesperson's date of purchase at not less than 90 percent of the salesperson's original net cost." This also applies to company-produced promotional materials, sales aids, or kits.

Still Unsure?

If you're thinking of signing on with a company, but aren't quite sure yet if this is right for you, contact the company and ask to attend a party in your area. See how potential customers interact with the product. If you can't attend a party, ask to talk to a couple of reps in your area to see how they're doing. Every legitimate company will gladly provide someone to answer your questions, so don't be shy.

Not long ago after a segment on starting a direct-sales business, the response on the *Good Morning America* message boards and through e-mail proved that many viewers were eager to tap into this opportunity, while others were already doing it and looking for ways to grow their businesses. To get beyond the median income, take into account that you'll have to work at building your business every day. Do you have the time and interest to devote to that? You'll have to reach out to new people all the time. Are you easily able to make new contacts from whom you'll ask for their business?

Other Questions to Ask

- Must I maintain a minimum sales volume to remain active? What happens if I fall below that minimum or need to take time off?

- What type of training do you provide? (You might receive training manuals and DVDs. You might have access to online tutorials.)

- Is ongoing support available? What format is such support provided in (phone, in-person, online, printed material)?

- What is the median income of your sellers? (Don't ask, "How much can I make?" since you'll be told the earning potential is unlimited.)

- How often are new products introduced?

- Will I deliver the merchandise to my customers or do you ship it directly to them?

- What is your buyback policy if I'm not satisfied with the opportunity?

Successful sellers think about their business all the time. They expect to work hard to generate an income; it doesn't happen on its own.

Do something daily. We spoke to hundreds of women who are in the $20,000-a-year bracket and each of them say they've reached that milestone because they contribute to their business daily. They don't just dream about making money, they take action every single day to make that money a reality. It could be contacting customers about reorders. It may be networking and socializing outside of their homes where they always talk about their business. For some it's as simple as meeting someone new at the hair salon and passing out business cards.

Just about everyone says they're constantly focused on planning future parties because the primary sales forum is getting friends to host parties, where people are invited to socialize and shop. Bottom line: Work isn't just on their minds, it's also in their actions.

This follows the direction once offered by the late Mary Kay

Happy at Home

"I became a Mary Kay independent beauty consultant in February 1989 as a way to make the $200 extra I needed to put my children in day care. At the time, I had a very demanding full-time corporate job as a National Marketing Manager, two toddlers under three years old, and was going through a divorce from my first husband. I needed more money as a soon-to-be single parent, but didn't want a part-time job that would take me away from my children for minimum wage.

"I attended a skin-care class and saw the Mary Kay opportunity first as a way to make more money in less time, and then later as a way to be a stay-at-home mom making an executive annual compensation.

"More than nineteen years later, I am one of only four independent national sales directors at the highest level of Mary Kay, making well over half a million dollars per year. My success comes from positioning myself with strong mentors and focusing on: maximizing the marketing plan, developing a skill-based business with an emphasis on strong people skills, discipline in doing the daily activities, purposeful and strategic goal-setting, and having persistence through obstacles."

—Gloria Mayfield Banks, Maryland

Ash, who would motivate her sales force to maintain written lists of the six most important things to do each day. The focus then was on achieving daily accomplishments, just as it is today.

Form a team. Many women who are making in excess of $2,000 a month have found that they're so passionate about direct sales, they want to form teams of other direct-sales representatives. These women become team leaders and they recruit friends to become independent sales reps who report in under them. This means they've now taken on two roles: They continue to sell, and they also motivate and lead their team. By managing a team, you make commission on the sales of your recruits.

Yet, it's not a walk in the park: As a leader, you're now doing

Happy at Home

"I chose the direct-sales business model because relationships are so important to me. Rubber stamping is a rewarding pastime that allows everyone to feel creative and fulfilled, even people who aren't instinctively artistic. The two (direct sales and stamps) are an ideal combination because direct sales provides the way for us to individually teach and demonstrate the art of stamping, an approach that is much more effective than when people simply buy stamps off the shelf at a store.

"As with many direct-sales companies, Stampin' Up! provides our independent demonstrators with flexibility and control over their own businesses. We welcome demonstrators who want to participate at any level, and our business model allows them to adjust their time commitment to individual circumstances. In addition, Stampin' Up! distinguishes itself because of the product we offer. Stamps are fun; stamping is personally rewarding and offers a wonderful social outlet. Our demonstrators join us because of the friends they have found and the gratifying feeling they enjoy as they create and share cards, scrapbook pages, gifts, home décor, and other handstamped projects."

—Shelli Gardner, Utah

your own sales, worrying about your own customers, and you're also motivating your team to achieve their sales goals.

In many ways, this mirrors the traditional workforce: Every manager knows that his or her direct reports have different motivators. Some people work hard to get a promotion. Some perform just to keep their jobs. Others work hard to make more money. In direct sales, people get into it for different reasons: to save for the holidays, to earn a vacation, to pay for home repairs, or to socialize. A great team leader recognizes that she'll have to know what motivates her team and she has to work to meet their needs. It's not just about signing people up to make more commission.

Bridging the gap. For some people, a desire to work at home may just be a temporary need, especially if they are taking care of children or an older parent, but they plan to return to a traditional office one day.

Happy at Home

"I started Luxe Jewels to help women find an alternative to the nine-to-five job. Women, especially moms, yearn for flexible hours and are natural entrepreneurs (they can juggle it all!). The idea of home party–based businesses is attractive to many women, but the reality of cheesy presentations and hard-to-sell items discourages many from trying. Luxe is different because our products are gorgeous, high-quality, and stylish—jewelry that our consultants are proud to wear and sell. The Luxe party is also a real party. There are no presentations: Just set up a display—really an in-home boutique—and let the guests mingle and try on the jewelry. Women with home-party sales experience are attracted to Luxe not only for the product, but also for our excellent, highly competitive compensation plan and the opportunity to get in on the ground floor of a new direct sales company with tons of potential."

—Jessica Herrin, California

Direct sales can be an ideal way to bridge the gap in employment. Starting a direct-selling business and forming a team not only means good money, but it builds invaluable leadership skills that many people can leverage into corporate careers. This is a way for anyone who wants to be at home to keep their hand in making money and building professional skills. This can make it easier to re-enter the workforce later if desired.

It's all about how you spin it. Building a customer base by selling cosmetics or gourmet food where you consistently raise the bar on your financial goals is something that any employer can relate to. Direct sales is also a smart way to maintain contact with a personal and professional network.

Happy at Home

"After adopting our first child, I decided to stay home. My husband, Curt, a CPA, supported my decision but asked me to contribute financially from home. I had always loved candles and fragrance, so I decided to make candles in my kitchen and sell them to friends to generate extra income. I thought it would be easy! It took me two years to perfect my first candle—to get the fragrance, wicks, and wax just right. The result was a clean-burning candle that permeated my home with a rich fragrance and warm ambience. That was June of 1997. In creating Gold Canyon, I had found a way to pursue a career that would allow me to be home with my children. I wanted Gold Canyon to offer this fulfilling opportunity to other women, and in doing so, we established a direct-selling business model. Soon, I discovered people not only loved the exquisitely fragrant candles but also the opportunity that came with it—the flexibility of a home-based business and selling a quality product they could believe in. Today, more than 25,000 independent demonstrators in the U.S., Canada, and the U.K. have fulfilled their own dreams through Gold Canyon."

—Karen Waisath, Arizona

ACTION STEPS

1. *If you've never been in sales,* write down five characteristics that you believe will help you excel in sales and ask three people close to you if they agree. Sales is tough and you have to be, too.

2. *Think hard about how much money you expect to make every month in direct sales.* Now reduce it by a third and see if this still seems viable. We suggest reducing it by a third because most people overestimate by one-half or two-thirds what they think they'll make. You may make twice what you expect the first month out, but chances are it will take a while, so make your decision based on more conservative numbers.

3. *Spend a half hour a day for two* weeks reading about direct sales and reviewing websites from companies you're considering. There is a great deal to digest, and a great deal to reject out there.

4. *Identify a couple of people who have made it in direct sales (whether from home or not).* Ask a lot of questions, including how many things they tried before they settled on a product/company to represent.

5. *If you attend a party or* event by an offering company, take a trusted companion along. Ideally this is someone who may hear things you don't in the presentation, and who can provide thoughtful feedback to your concerns and/or interest in a company.

■ ■ ■

chapter seven

Found Money:
Pocket Change for Life's Extras

Depending on your age, you may remember your mother referring to "mad money" or "pin money." Both are old-fashioned but charming terms for that little stash of cash women squirrel away for special purposes.

This isn't money to pay the mortgage or the grocery bill. We're talking fun money for holiday gifts, a special trip, or family vacations. Maybe it's to fund date nights with your spouse. It's stuff for you, your family, and your lifestyle.

Whatever your more regular source of income, you have decided that you could use a little bit more. We've got smart ideas to inspire you with the confidence to move forward.

It's All About You

Extra earning is all about you—your interests, your contacts, and your schedule. Whether you're a student with a full course load, a new mom with hours to fill during nap time, or a boomer not yet ready to hang it up, there's a way to bring in money without committing to full-time work.

We've identified two types of opportunities: online and in-person, both with pros and cons depending on your situation. If you're tied to your house because you're caring for a parent or a child, or perhaps because you have physical or emotional challenges that prevent you from leaving home, online possibilities will make the most sense. If you're bored to tears within your own four walls and need a change of scenery while the kids are in school, you'll want to get out and about.

Before you run for the phone or start clicking, ask and answer a few questions that will get you on the right path:

- What's your purpose? Do you want to earn $250 a week? Or would you settle for that amount per month? Do you want to remember how good it felt to have some of your very own money to spend, no matter what the amount?

- How much time do you have? Although this type of work is all about flexibility, you should decide roughly how much time you'll spend earning each week.

- What will it cost you? If delivering newspapers for two hours a day makes sense, be sure to factor in the gas and the wear and tear on your car. It's got to be worth your time.

- What will you do with the money? Again, you don't have to spell this out precisely, but knowing what you're aiming toward will keep you focused and motivated.

Online Opportunities

Be a Mystery Shopper. Mystery shoppers may not make a ton of money, but they get to do what they love—dine out and shop! Businesses want to know what the experiences of average customers are like so they can improve the shopping experience. That's why they hire mystery shoppers to anonymously visit establishments, then report back on the level of service, cleanliness, and timeliness.

Mystery shoppers are paid in cash or in freebies. Few people make a living at this, so we don't recommend relying on it to pay the bills. Beware—some organizations will ask you to pay to become a mystery shopper. In most cases, a legitimate opportunity will not cost you anything. Learn more at MysteryShop.org.

Channel Your Inner Judge Judy. There's an interesting occasional-work category known as e-juror or online juror. Lawyers deciding whether or not to accept a case or looking for feedback on cases they're currently handling turn to specialized services that deliver cost-effective research and focus groups online. These give lawyers an opportunity to test their legal theories in a mock trial before heading into a live courtroom.

Online jurors receive a fee for their participation. The amount can range from $10 to $100, depending on the length of the e-trial. Among sites to consult are OnlineVerdict.com, ZapJury.com, and TrialPrac tice.com.

Drive for Dollars. Have you seen those wrapped cars that carry advertising? They're often driven by people who want to earn pocket money while driving around as they normally would. There are a number of companies that look for people to advertise for their clients. Call around. Don't settle on the first yes you get, as there may be a more lucrative opportunity available. We've seen estimates of around $300 a month, providing that you meet the criteria, which can include driving about 1,000 miles a month, washing the car regularly, and sometimes parking on the street.

Check out DrivingPromotions.com and AutoWrapped.com to learn about this industry. (Although the work is not done virtually, you'll find the contacts online by searching under keywords "car wrap advertising.")

Get Published and Paid. Some websites pay for articles and reviews, but unless they're commissioning your original work, you won't make a great deal of money. For example, Associatedcontent.com, a large site with articles about nearly everything, pays about $10 per approved and

Happy at Home

"ChaCha is a completely different way to search the Internet. Instead of going to a website, typing in what you're trying to find, and then becoming aggravated after searching without any relevant results, ChaCha allows you to search with an expert guide who can assist you with your search.

"That is where I come in! As an official guide, I help people (in the ChaCha world, referred to as "info seekers") search for whatever they are looking for. Sounds easy, right? Well, it is. Not only that, but it's something you can do at any hour of the day, when you happen to have free time. You also have the opportunity to search topics you are generally interested and knowledgeable about.

"ChaCha pays me $10 per search hour so basically I choose how much I want to make. I can also invite other people to become guides.

"I absolutely love working from the comfort of home. There is no stress to deal with, and no traffic to fight while commuting to work. If I cannot sleep, I can get up for a while and work. I never worry about paying high gas prices, unlike most people who have to commute to work. I'm always busy helping students with their school assignments. I am amazed at the never-ending learning experience that comes with searching. I never get bored with ChaCha."

—Donna Kanagy, West Virginia

published piece. Helium.com and MyEssays.com pay about $10 to $100 for accepted work depending on length. There's more on this category at WriterFind.com. At ReviewMe.com, PayPerPost.com, Blog gingAds.com, and other similar sites, you can get paid for your blogs.

Guide Online Searches. Everybody knows how Internet search engines work. You type in what you want to know and answers appear. A company called ChaCha combines traditional search engine technology with free, live assistance to help users get the precise results they want. The company hires and trains guides who love to learn, have great communication skills, embrace new technology, are service-focused, and are knowledgeable about specific topics. Sound like anyone you know? Get details at ChaCha.com and Mahalo.com.

Tutor in Cyberspace. Parents are embracing online tutoring because it's ultraconvenient—no more driving your student to the tutor's home or finding time for the tutor to come to you. Now, many companies are using online tutors, generally college graduates or current students, with expertise in English, math, science, social studies, and other subjects. Check out sites including Tutor.com, Care.com, TutorVista.com, eSylvan.com, and BrainFuse.com.

In-Person Opportunities

The world moves so fast these days and people are so busy, it's no wonder there's a thriving market for products and services that make life easier and more convenient. That's the idea behind a lot of great schemes for making extra money: doing something someone else could probably do but doesn't have the time for.

The great thing about this at-home category is that it's basically without rules and limits. If you know someone who's expressed an interest in receiving a homemade, vegetarian casserole twice a week, you're in business. You've invested nearly nothing in your start-up, and if you charge properly, you'll make some extra cash. Who knows, you might just find another customer or two who wants to offer her family a healthy meal but doesn't have time to prepare it. Suddenly, you're really in business.

Convert Clutter to Cash. This is an idea that's been around as long as clutter, but there are new ways to pursue it. The traditional strategy is to hold a garage sale. These are always more fun to do with a friend or neighbor. Our good friend Catherine held them all the time when her children were young and constantly outgrowing everything. She always made sure to have a free bin. It was filled with items she could never get much cash for, but people loved the idea of free.

Another way to do this is by selling a boat, car, lawn mower, exercise equipment, unused jewelry, or other items of value. You not only get some fast cash in your hand, you also reduce lawn or garage clutter and recycle usable goods.

CraigsList.com is an excellent way to go. It's the website that offers mostly free classifieds. Alternately, newspaper classifieds, neighborhood/grocery store bulletin boards, and e-mail lists are other ways to make your offerings known.

Errand Runner. If you're new to the workforce, or have been out a while, consider offering a simple service—running errands. Charge $10 to $15 an hour when you are getting started, but remember to consider the cost of gas. Seniors are a ready resource for your services, but young families with two working parents need help, too. Prepare a simple brochure or e-flyer to discuss your services; be sure to include a testimonial from a satisfied customer.

Family Assistant. To understate the situation, today's working parents are on overload. They're holding down full-time (plus) jobs, raising kids, and managing busy households. An entrepreneurial, reliable family assistant can be a huge help—running errands, driving the kids to music lessons, or meeting service people at the house. You could be hired to organize the pantry, pack away last season's clothes, or open the door for the cable guy.

If you know someone who you think could use this kind of help, don't hesitate to recommend yourself. Because it's not that common, people may not consider it as they would hiring someone to help with housecleaning or landscaping.

To keep things simple, establish an hourly rate to cover all tasks. Be sure the rate is adequate to cover your time and gas. Set your boundaries from the outset. If, for example, you do not wish to deal with food or infants, make that clear.

Flower Arranging. Do guests always admire your flower-arranging skills? This is a great way to make some extra money. Start-up costs are minimal—vases and flowers. You may wish to send an e-flyer or, if you can do it affordably, develop a simple website and showcase arrangements for Mother's Day, weddings, Valentine's Day, and other big flower occasions. You will also need to arrange for inexpensive transportation. Market yourself to neighbors, friends, party planners, and small businesses.

Monogramming. This is a great part-time business. You can set this business up right in your own home. Promote the business at craft shows and through flyers. Also try ads in local newspapers. Monogramming and embroidering are often used synonymously. In today's world, more and more people wish to distinguish themselves from others. One effective way is to identify personal items with initials. This includes purses, towels, hats, and other articles personalized with business logos, names, or initials. The size of your investment (equipment to digitally perform the work) will depend on the kinds of items you wish to monogram. There is plenty of information available online to better acquaint you with monogramming and embroidering business opportunities. Check out the online publication ImpressionsMag.com.

Newborn Needs. Another life passage that can put people over the edge is the presence of a new baby. Especially if the family lives far from the couple's parents, the need for extra help is significant. And even if the family has hired a nurse or a nanny, there are endless tasks that need doing. Shopping for groceries and diapers, putting in extra loads of laundry, dropping off older kids to play dates, exchanging gifts— everything that lets the new parents spend time with the baby.

Office Assistant/Gal Friday. This category is similar to family assistant, but is focused more on office tasks you can do from home. Small business owners have to wear many hats and often need help typing documents, conducting Internet research, booking travel, or making follow-up phone calls to customers.

You may be called on to make a run to the office store or warehouse club to purchase supplies. Or you may be needed to pick up visitors from the airport and deliver them to a hotel or meeting place. You may also be asked to come into the office or shop from time to time to help with filing and answering the phone. Small business owners love knowing they can rely on you when things get crazy!

Scrapbook Suzie. This is a good business idea that you can market to your immediate circle of friends. People love scrapbooks, but most of us just don't have the time to devote to them, though they love the idea of capturing memories and moments in this way. Scrapbook for those who can't! Clients provide you with the photographs, clippings, and other materials, and you design the books. Since scrapbooking is labor intensive, determine how long it takes you to produce an average-sized scrapbook so you have a good idea of your hourly investment of time. Build your hourly rate on that. You may wish to quote a project fee once you can determine with accuracy the time it will take to do various projects. There's more at ScrapBook.com and ScrapBooking.com.

Second Home Caretaker. Do you live year round in a beach area or other vacation community? If so, consider marketing your services to those who own homes but are not permanent residents. This could be anything from watching over the property to overseeing repairs, watering plants, or stocking the pantry and fridge before the owners arrive. You're not a property manager, you're more of a caretaker, the eyes and ears of the out-of-town owner. This is one of those peace-of-mind jobs; the presence of a trusted person can be invaluable to long-distance property owners.

Seize the Season. The holiday season from Thanksgiving through New Year's is over-the-top busy for most people. Planning parties, preparing special meals, organizing trips, and buying and wrapping gifts can be overwhelming, especially on top of work, family duties, and volunteering.

That's where you come in. The possibilities for ambitious, energetic people with transportation and some time on their hands are endless. Consider these:

• **Trim-a-Tree.** Work with your client to select a theme (yesteryear . . . Cybertree . . . family tree) and decorate a beautiful, memorable Christmas tree. Use existing ornaments or supplement as needed—whatever's required to achieve the magic.

- **Send in the Sweets.** Everybody loves a tin of homemade cookies during the holidays. Bake and sell these to be used as gifts, hostess favors, or just to have around the house. Choose recipes that freeze well to increase your efficiency. Tuesday afternoon is gingerbread, Wednesday morning is decorated sugar cookies, and so on. You get the idea.

- **Cope with the Cards.** Getting cards selected, printed, addressed, stamped, and in the mail is no small task. If you have beautiful handwriting or can do calligraphy, you may just land yourself a gig addressing. Otherwise, use your word-processing, mail-merge, and envelope-stuffing skills.

- **Brave the Malls.** If you're a confident shopper, who isn't bothered by crowded malls, why not take someone's list and competently deliver everything on it? This may involve driving to a specialty store on the other side of town, shopping online, or sourcing a hard-to-find gift. Good communication skills and responsible judgment are important to ensure you're buying what someone else is envisioning.

- **Be a Party Smarty.** Planning a holiday party is not for the faint of heart. You need solid experience with food, venues, entertainment, and managing the unanticipated. If you can do it, there's no better time of year to offer your services.

- **Elf Anyone?** An all-purpose assistant can be a dream come true this time of year. Establish an hourly rate and offer generic services—an extra pair of hands to be used as the client wishes. Approach someone you know who does a significant amount of holiday preparation and entertaining. Be cheerful and hard-working, like all good elves.

Sell It on eBay. One smart friend started buying up sale merchandise from upscale department stores and selling it on eBay. Today her house has been taken over by merchandise and packing materials, but she's having a great time making money.

Whether you love shopping for antiques, clothing, or household goods, eBay lets you sell from home. A recent eBay/Nielsen survey found the average U.S. household has 52 unused items valued at $3200 just lying around. Scoop up your old stuff and sell it on eBay. See what's involved at eBay.com, and if you need live assistance, see ebay.com/ta.

Serve Seniors. The graying of the baby boom generation has resulted in an explosion in the number of people sixty-five and older in this country. Although many remain healthy and productive and need no immediate assistance, others require help. The desire among many seniors to remain independent is strong. That means there's a very real need for the types of assistance that keeps people in their homes.

We're not talking about medical care here, but tasks like organizing medication and making sure it's taken, getting the mail, preparing a simple meal, or changing a lightbulb. One woman makes consistent cash by phoning a list of seniors every morning. She makes sure all is well and reports back by e-mail to the seniors' adult children. They are secure in the knowledge that their parents are well, and she gets a consistent, though not bank-busting, income.

Another entrepreneur has a nice little business shopping for seniors. She takes their lists, usually over the phone, delivers the groceries and even puts them away if that's desired.

The value of this type of outreach is often as much in the socialization as in the task performed. So if you enjoy spending time with older people, this can be satisfying occasional work. The hours can vary. You might be needed for an hour a day seven days a week, or perhaps a couple of hours on Saturday and Sunday when other resources are not available.

For possible leads, reach out to a local hospital or your place of worship. Inquire among friends who help care for elderly parents and may need an extra pair of hands.

Wedding Warrior. Weddings are tough to pull off and a little extra, affordable help can go a long way toward happily ever after for everybody involved. Many brides hire wedding planners—event specialists who can plan and execute all major aspects of a wedding from getting the band and working with caterers to arranging fittings and planning the honeymoon. But the service can be quite costly and many brides and families just can't afford it.

If you adore weddings and recently had or planned one, you may like to offer yourself as a wedding assistant. Duties can be as diverse as you can imagine—from stuffing invitations into envelopes to rolling silverware for the reception, returning unwanted gifts, driving out-of-town guests around, and dozens more possibilities.

Charge reasonably, be efficient, and stay calm when everyone else is losing their heads. That combination can earn you some money *and* a recommendation. Talk with the owners of bridal shops, florists, or catering halls in your area. Tell them what you're doing and ask if you can place flyers or leave business cards in their spaces.

Thoughts on Pricing

As an independent contractor, which is what you'll be as an occasional worker, you can charge by the hour or by the project. You may find that a project fee works better in some cases. An example is a large, intensive job for which you don't want to have to account for every five-minute phone call. The challenge here is undercharging. Think carefully before you propose a sum. You can always go down if the circumstances warrant, but you can't easily go up.

Even if you charge a fixed fee for the project, you need to do it based on an hourly rate. In order to determine the overall cost of the job, you'll need to know approximately how many hours will be involved and about how much money you hope to make per hour.

Also do your homework to learn if there's anyone else in your community doing something similar and, if so, what she is charging.

You may have to amend your hourly rate based on other factors, including your experience. If you're a registered nurse establishing a senior assistant business, you may be able to charge more than someone with no medical background.

Finally, remember that when it comes to pricing, you don't have to be the cheapest to get the business, even if you're new. You just have to be good, reliable, and easy to work with.

ACTION STEPS

1. *If you're not sure how you'd like to make money, check the big online job boards for inspiration* (HotJobs.com, CareerBuilder.com and Monster .com); see what's in demand in your area using your skills. Even if the listings are for full-time work, many ideas can be converted into occasional opportunities.

2. *Sit down with your family or three best friends* and tell them you're considering starting your own home-based enterprise to fund little extras. See what ideas they suggest. Knowing you and your strengths, they can help generate some great ideas.

3. *Determine how much money you want to make and how much time you have to give.* This is sometimes a hard issue to balance. We will want to make as much money as possible in as little time as needed. But the reality doesn't work that way.

4. *Once you've decided what you're doing, offer free or discounted service for a limited time to a client or two.* This is your beta test, an opportunity to work out the kinks in your plan. It's hard to resist free and if you're good, they'll be happy to pay you next time.

5. *Don't be afraid to multitask.* To many women, multitasking is like breathing. So maybe you bake Christmas cookies *and* haul kids around to after-school appointments. Efficiency is what it's all about, whatever the task.

6. *Consider partnering with a friend.* You may have complementary skills or just enjoy doing things together. What's more, two of you can reach more people and be more responsive than you alone. Of course, profit must be divided, too, but you'll probably attract more business based on each of your connections.

■ ■ ■

chapter eight

Scam Busters

While thinking about making money, it's also important to pay particular attention to how to avoid losing it, too. While there are many legitimate ways to make money at home, there are also plenty of scammers out there. Christine Durst, founder of RatRace Rebellion.com, says her research indicates the ratio of scams to legitimate opportunities is forty-eight to one.

We Tried This at Home

As part of our research, we decided to put envelope stuffing to the test. We responded to ads to stuff envelopes that boasted the ability to earn up to $1,500 a week with little effort. Though we were of course very skeptical, we took a chance and bought about a dozen different starter kits for $20 to $50 each, figuring one might work. Each instructed us to mail flyers aimed at recruiting other people to stuff envelopes. We weren't being asked to promote a product or service—we were just told to get other people to stuff envelopes with the same offer. If they purchased the same kit, we would receive a commission.

Not to brag, but we're both awfully resourceful, yet neither of us could get this opportunity to pan out. Not a single cent. Recruiting people to stuff envelopes is the oldest work-from-home gimmick that fools people every day. Don't be one of them.

That isn't to say that all home-based opportunities that request money up-front are rip-offs. Many legitimate direct sales companies and others that help you start your own business or offer you an opportunity to make money require a start-up fee to cover the cost of training manuals and supplies to get you going. This could range from a couple hundred dollars to more than a few thousand dollars. The purpose of the up-front costs is often to weed out people who aren't serious. The theory is that those who are willing to invest their own money in getting their home-based opportunity off the ground are less likely to quit after only a few weeks or throw in the towel when the going gets tough. They tend to stick it out for the long haul, and they wind up successful because of it.

We've also tried to find legitimate craft assembly work, but have always come up empty-handed. The ads promise that you'll learn how to put together adorable little craft projects and then sell them for a profit. The catch: There's no market for your wares. Nobody wants to buy them. And no company will pay you for them either, no matter how much they promise to do so.

Do This Before You Pay

Before submitting a credit card payment after reading hype on a website, consider a few key pointers:

Watch the wording. Imagine you see an ad that boasts, "Earn up to $1,500 a week! No skills required!" Gee, wouldn't that be nice? Who wouldn't want to jump at the chance? But before you're tempted to say, "Sign me up," put on your logic cap for a moment. Is it really and truly possible that someone would pay you such big bucks while at the same time announcing that it didn't matter if you were a dummy?

Time and again we receive e-mails from disappointed victims who say they were scammed by such lofty promises. They paid upward of $100 for a starter kit, only to discover they weren't going to make a penny, let alone anything close to $1,500 a week. The disappointed buyers realize they were duped, and they're most upset because they have only themselves to blame for being gullible. Apply loads of common sense when evaluating possible offers.

Never send money if you can't talk to a person. If there's no phone number on the website, but the person, advertisement, or company is promising you big bucks, simply stay away. You may have to apply online before talking to someone, but you shouldn't send money to someone you can't talk to. Ask what specifically you'll be required to do. Ask for the company to describe a typical work day to you. Find out what tasks you must perform or accomplish to get paid. Is pay by commission or salary? Ask about the realistic earning potential and about the obstacles and challenges, too.

If you wanted to become a consultant with Mary Kay or Avon, you would have absolutely no trouble finding people willing to talk—not just e-mail you—about how to get started. The same access to information and people should be your standard for any home-based opportunity you consider.

Inquire about money-back policies. If you are going to send money, ask first about a money-back guarantee. Specifically, find out how you will have to go about requesting a refund if you're not satisfied and when you will receive it. This is especially important for websites that require a registration fee for access to listings or for sites that want to sell you an "information packet" or "starter kit." If there is no money-back policy, then decide on your own if you're willing to take a risk in the event the materials aren't what you had hoped they would be.

Do your due diligence. In just a few simple steps—both online and via phone—you can learn a lot about a company or opportunity.

- Start by searching the Internet for any information on the company. You might find entries on message boards that praise and/or complain about the company. Read such material with a grain of salt: Someone could be getting paid to say good things that aren't necessarily true, while others may have an unfair ax to grind. Yet it's better to review such material before making an investment, even a nominal one, instead of after the fact.

- Check with the Better Business Bureau (BBB.org) for any complaints about the company. The absence of information registered with the Bureau doesn't necessarily mean the company is legit, but many negatives could be a red flag.

- Try to verify the seller's PayPal record before sending a dime. Many scammers require you to submit payment via a PayPal account, but research online and see if they have negative comments registered against them. This is similar to a seller's or buyer's eBay feedback.

- Visit the Federal Trade Commission's website (FTC.gov) for tips and numbers for registering complaints. Similarly, if you have been scammed, be sure to report the nature of your complaint to these outlets as well.

- Even though a company may provide references, use your intuition to know if they're legit. Think about it: Anyone can find someone to say something nice, even if it's not true. So don't settle for just one or two references. Find several who'll answer your questions to your satisfaction.

- Before signing employment agreements or independent contractor documents, read every word carefully. If you don't understand something, ask for clarification or seek the advice of a lawyer. If it's so complicated that you don't get it, that's a red flag. Be confident about every word before committing.

When evaluating job postings and work-at-home advertisements, look for some signs that are often warnings of potential trouble. These may include:

- Promises of unlimited earning potential with no skills needed.

- Spelling mistakes and grammatical errors.

- An e-mail address that doesn't include the company name as the primary domain.

- Words and phrases such as money transfers, wiring funds, packaging, forwarding, check cashing, lottery redemption, foreign agent, and overseas contact.

Do Not Reveal
Secure Information

Once you've accepted a job and you opt for direct deposit, you will have to provide your bank account number. But this information is not relevant in the application process. Beyond that, you should never reveal passwords and PIN numbers for banking information or PayPal accounts, even though many seemingly professional online sites request these details. Such sites claim they only request such information to determine if you're an honest applicant. Don't fall for that nonsense. No legitimate operation will ever ask for your banking passwords or PIN numbers.

Don't Be Too Quick to Say Yes

Just because an ad or posting for a work-at-home opportunity appears on a seemingly reputable website doesn't mean the opportunity has been verified for legitimacy. The big job boards and a wide range of work-from-home websites are rich in resources. Yet they often feature ads and links, especially those posted through Google's AdSense network, that aren't vetted for accuracy. With an abundance of opportunities out there, no single source can possibly verify the validity of every opportunity. You must do your own

Beware: Unhappy at Home

"My husband and I received a letter in the mail claiming that I had won the International Lottery. It looked like an official letter with a check addressed to me for $114,000. I was skeptical at first, but we took it to our bank in Tampa, Florida. The manager confirmed that the letter and check appeared legitimate.

"We deposited the money into our checking account, spent some of it, only to discover it was fraudulent. The bank closed our checking account and froze all of our assets. We were responsible for repaying the money, which has been absolutely devastating.

"I don't wish this on anyone. Even if the check looks real, don't believe it. Don't fall for foreign lottery games or check-cashing schemes. They'll get you every time."

—Geena Harris, Florida

research, inject a big dose of common sense, and follow the advice here to avoid getting ripped off.

In the end, only you can decide if an opportunity is right for you. I wouldn't be willing to pay money in hopes of making money unless I could talk to someone about all of my questions and concerns—the good, bad, and ugly. Remember, some people make thousands of dollars selling cosmetics and they're rewarded with pink Cadillacs. Even though Mary Kay is a legitimate company with an honorable money-making opportunity, that doesn't mean it is for everyone. Plenty of people fail at peddling lipsticks and blush.

The same theory holds true for every single home-based opportunity. Just as some people may thrive while working from home, other people would be driven insane if they couldn't get out of the house. What might be one person's dream is another person's nightmare. Even with legitimate possibilities, only you can decide if it's right for you.

ACTION STEPS

Dissect the wording of several advertisements or job descriptions to be sure you understand the real opportunity. Ask a spouse or trusted friend to review your conclusions.

1. *Research the offering company* thoroughly to determine any relevant history, including successes and complaints.

2. *Ask about a money-back guarantee* and make careful notes of the answer, including the person you spoke or e-mailed with.

3. *Identify at least three people* involved in direct sales, ideally in the industry you're considering. Ask questions and learn all you can about the opportunity.

■ ▦ ▪

chapter nine

Setting Up Shop

Ever felt envious of those photos in the decorating magazines? You know, the ones of charming home offices furnished in warm woods and neutral tones where everything fits into a cubby and not a sheet of paper is out of place? Where the woman behind the desk—in chic yet comfy clothes—looks like she could land a huge deal, quiet a toddler's tantrum, and get supper on the table all without breaking a sweat?

Do these images represent a work-at-home fantasy or a blueprint for your future? We think the answer lies somewhere in between. With thoughtful planning, ingenuity, and a modest budget you can establish a professional work environment you'll love spending time in. An office with the décor, equipment, and karma you need to succeed.

Will a great space help you attract work and pull it off brilliantly? Maybe not directly. But the right HQ for your business *will* make you feel good about yourself and your decision. That can lead to greater confidence and more energy. And no matter what kind of work you're pursuing, confidence and energy will always help you do it better.

Yours—All Yours

If you're like most of us, your past work spaces have not been of your choosing. Now you can finally have one that's uniquely you. Create a space that reflects your personality, goals, and interests.

Hang that embroidered sampler your grandmother made in 1940. Cover a wall with corkboard and create a montage of family photos. Buy a one-cup water heater and make herbal tea whenever you want.

Whatever the size or personality of your space, it's essential to separate it from your home life. Think about it. Do you want to be sitting at the computer at 11:00 P.M. answering e-mail? Do you want to hear the phone ringing with questions while you're bathing the baby or having dinner with the family? Probably not.

Set boundaries, including fixed working hours, mindful that there will be times when these will have to expand. Establish a general sense of when you're available to focus on work. For some people, it's nights and weekends. For others, it's chunks of time here and there throughout the seven days.

Plan with an eye to your own productivity style. If you are fresh and amazing in the morning and your family life can accommodate it, get cranking at 5:00 A.M. You can't make too many productive phone calls at that hour, but you certainly can create new product designs, reply to e-mail, and pay bills. Same goes for those who come alive after the sun goes down. Nine-to-five just doesn't work for everyone, and now that you're on your own, it doesn't have to.

Table the Idea

If you're serious about creating a home-based work life, the kitchen or dining room table is simply not going to cut it. You need a quiet, dedicated space where you can work uninterrupted. A place where you can feel as if you're at work, not like you're studying for a social studies test.

Space and budget constraints may make it impossible to start off with an office that doesn't do double duty as the kids' playroom. We certainly don't recommend you put your work-at-home dreams on hold while you create the ideal space. So do what you must to make it work.

If you're in direct sales or service, a small area of your bedroom, a landing, loft, or part of the living room might be sufficient for office space. But if you're working for a large company—for example, as a virtual customer service agent—you'll eventually want to set aside a room or space expressly for work. In fact, some employers require it. If your business will require storage of products or samples, you'll need to plan for this, too.

Think creatively—your unfinished basement may be little more than a dark storage area, but maybe it's time to give it a second look. A big carpet remnant and warm lighting can transform your cellar into a fledgling corporate headquarters. For just a couple hundred dollars, you can score a nice desk and some comfy chairs from Target.

Home Office Tips—Our
Two Cents

There's a lot to think about as you start to plan your home office. Consider these recommendations to enhance comfort and productivity.

Light your way to success. Choose a space with the maximum natural lighting. Then augment it with good task lighting that doesn't throw a glare onto your computer screen or work area. Good light helps prevent eyestrain and can help keep your mood positive.

Dare to decorate. You're going to be spending hour after hour in your work space. Select paint colors and artwork that make you feel good. And surround yourself with objects (not too many—clutter is an enemy of productivity) you love.

Get ergonomic. Ergonomics is the science that fits the job to the worker, rather than the worker to the job. An ergonomically designed office emphasizes comfort and helps you avoid excessive bending, lifting, or reaching. Frequently used files and equipment are at your fingertips. Background noise has been eliminated and you can work at ease for long stretches of time.

Optimize organization. Starting fresh is a great way to get and stay organized. First off, make sure business records are separate from your home files. This is important because home businesses definitely receive their share of IRS audits, especially if owners are writing off a portion of the mortgage or rent. Keep plenty of office supplies (computer paper, cartridges, file folders) on hand so productivity doesn't grind to a halt when you run out of something. And even if you're the only one in the office, keep your space looking as though your biggest client might walk through the door at any time.

Polish your professionalism. Even the smallest, newest business should make a strong professional impression. One simple strategy is to rent a post office box if you'd prefer that over using your home address for correspondence. If you can afford it, install a separate phone line and answering machine or voice mail service. Use an e-mail address that's professional, not personal. For example, JaneDoe@email.com is much better than BlondeMommy@email.com.

Other Great Ideas

There are so many wonderful ideas out there for creating a home office that's so you and so efficient. One of the best minds in the business belongs to Julie Morgenstern, author of *Organizing from the Inside Out*. She also runs a New York–based organizing business that helps put all kinds of people in shipshape—from small business owners to top executives.

One of Morgenstern's great contributions is the kindergarten classroom model. Huh?! You read right. Remember your kindergarten classroom? Okay, maybe your kids' kindergarten? There are distinct zones of activity—art, storytime, nap mats, snacks, and all the rest. Within each zone is everything you might need to do that activity. In the art area you'll find the paints, the clay, the apron and whatnot.

Same goes for your work space. If clients visit your space, you'll need a space to greet and visit with them. If you are actually producing a craft or other product, you need a production area that's distinct from the place from where you run the business. It's a wonderful concept and appealing in its simplicity. Her website is JulieMorgenstern.com.

Prepare for Takeoff

We also like the ideas promoted by organizer Liz Davenport. She recommends creating a cockpit at your desk. That means selecting the tools you use most often and bringing them within arm's reach.

The problem, she says, is that once you get up to fetch a needed item, you can be gone twenty minutes if you're not careful. If you use something more than once a month, store it in the office. If you use it less frequently, store it farther away.

The pilot analogy continues with Davenport's concept of creating an "air traffic control system" to keep order. The system is comprised of four tools: an in-box, a to-read file, a file file, and a hot file. The hot file is those files you touch every day or so—current clients, ongoing projects, or tasks you repeat frequently.

At least every twenty-four hours the boxes should be reviewed and emptied. Managing the files takes common sense and discipline. For example, if the to-read file gets filled with more than you can handle, pull out three to five important pieces and dump the rest, knowing you'll never get to it anyway.

According to Davenport, the average person wastes more than 150 hours every year looking for stuff they need to do their job. She says that's like losing almost a month a year just looking for what you need! Learn more at OrderfromChaos.com.

Plugging In

It's hard to envision any type of work that doesn't require a computer these days. Whether it's for record keeping, Internet research, or word processing, you need a good computer on your staff. And beyond the equipment itself, you'll probably need high-speed Internet access.

When it comes to hardware, we recommend these home-office basics:

- Computer, monitor, and printer
- High-speed Internet access

- Dedicated phone line with answering machine or service
- Fax/copier/scanner combination—optional, depending on your needs
- Telephone headset if you will spend considerable time on the phone
- Personal Digital Assistant—optional, depending on your needs.

Think in terms of tasks and goals. What computer tasks will you be doing immediately and what capacity will you need as your business grows?

If all you do is word process and use the Internet, a basic PC or Mac with an entry-level inkjet or laser printer might be all you need. If your business will demand sophisticated audio, graphic, or number-crunching capabilities, a higher level machine with color inkjet or laser printer is probably necessary. You should be able to outfit yourself with a basic computer and printer for $600 to $1,000 unless your needs are more sophisticated. And if you're taking your current job home, you can negotiate who is paying for services that you'll need in order to perform your responsibilities. Just because an employer is allowing you to work from home doesn't mean all of the costs must be covered at your expense. You should always ask if there's a monthly stipend or allowance provided or specifically what elements they'll cover.

Beyond the hardware, there are many types of software that help people work efficiently from home. These link users to their offices or make it possible to share information and conference with people across town or across the world.

Google Apps (Google.com/Apps) is an example. The company known for its search engine offers a suite of services including e-mail, instant messaging, calendar, and document-sharing. This is an essential service, which is free, if you're working with people in multiple locations and have to access the same documents. Another offering is Gotomypc.com. This program permits you to access an office computer and all its files and e-mail from a remote location, which is valuable if you travel.

Headset at Home

One of the most high-value office tools we know is a telephone headset. These are relatively inexpensive, easy-to-use devices that free your hands while you're on the phone. Perhaps most important, they prevent you from cradling the phone in an uncomfortable position that can result in neck and shoulder pain.

The principles of ergonomics dictate that equipment used for work should enhance the worker's comfort and productivity. The idea is to avoid awkward, unnatural postures (like the one required to hold a phone between your ear and shoulder while you're typing or writing).

There are wireless, cellular, and corded headsets, as well as those that wirelessly connect to your computer using USB ports, Bluetooth, and other technologies. There are on-the-ear, over-the-head, in-the-ear, and behind-the-neck models. Monaural headsets have only one ear pad, which lets you hear other people and sound while you're on the phone. Binaural models have two ear pads to block outside noise.

The headset you use may be influenced by the type of telephone system you have, such as traditional or VOIP (voice over Internet protocol, which basically is the routing of voice conversations over the Internet through any IP-based network). In some job situations, such as working as a virtual customer service agent, you may be required to use this type of over-the-computer phone system.

You can shop for headsets at office and electronics stores. There are also lots of good online resources including Plantronics.com, Headsets.com, Officeheadsets.com, and Amazon.com. Costs can range from under $100 and up. Some sets plug into your computer or existing phone, others come with their own telephone keypads.

Be Prepared

One of the perks most missed by people who make the transition to a home-based office is the tech support. Being able to summon free assistance with a quick call or e-mail is a thing of the past once you're on your own.

Lining up help for those painful, panicky moments *before* things start falling apart is essential. There are a number of options, including services like GeeksOnTime.com, GeekSquad.com, Computer Assistant.com, PlumChoice.com, SupportFreaks.com, and Support .com. Before deciding on one of these, compare hourly rates, phone vs. in-person support, hours of operation, and package rates.

Other options:

- Call the computer science department of a nearby college. Find out if they have a job board that lists names of tech-savvy students who do installation and repairs. If you go this route, you may have to sacrifice speed and convenience.

- Consider bartering computer help with a service you can provide someone else. Here, too, you'll want to be sure your provider is highly reliable.

- Contact the manager of your local computer store to see if some knowledgeable employees do freelance in-home repair work.

Check references before inviting someone you don't know into your home.

Going Live

Establishing a website can be easy and inexpensive. Whatever the product or service, good websites add credibility and visibility to your home-based business. Alternately, an unprofessional site can make your enterprise look like a lemonade stand. So choose your strategy and support carefully. The good news is you don't have to be a webmaster with lots of fancy equipment to create an impressive site.

Here are the basic steps to create a website for your new business:

- *Spend time online looking at the websites of competing or similar businesses.* Make a list of what you like and don't like, including how they're written, how they're designed, and how easy or difficult they are to navigate.

- *Choose an ISP (Internet service provider).* This is something you have to do anyway to line up regular Internet service. You'll want a competitive price that includes e-mail, file transfer capability, and server space for a website.

- *Choose and register a website or domain name.* The name should be appealing, should reflect what you're doing, and should be easy to remember. Search the web first to be sure the one you want isn't taken, then do a trademark search. The U.S. Patent and Trademark Office has a free search tool at USPTO.gov. Then search WhoIs.com (or another ISP) to see if what you want is available. The cost of registering a domain name starts at as little as $10 per year. If the name you want is available, go ahead and buy it even if you're not quite ready. That way it will be there when you decide it's time to create the site.

- *Dig into design.* For some people, a web consultant, designer, and developer are needed. Design costs are based on the amount of content, site features, and complexity. That makes a reasonable cost estimate difficult. But a bare bones approach (basically an online flyer without much interactive capability) can be yours for a very modest sum. You can even create that yourself.

- *Host and maintain.* The site must be hosted on a server. A simple website can cost under $10 a month to host, but a site where you're doing business online (e-commerce) can cost much more. Look carefully for hosting services with strong track records and relatively little down time. The cost of maintenance will vary according to the simplicity or complexity of the changes. Your web designer should be able to do maintenance, but get a firm idea of costs before agreeing to anything.

There are also some free resources for web design. Open Source Web Design's website (OSWD.org) offers free templates and can be a great place to start.

- *Stay on top.* Even if you outsource hosting and maintenance services, you need to be proactive to keep your site fresh and viable. That can include making sure content (products, pricing, success stories, news) is up-to-date and following up on e-mail that comes through the site. If you have tracking software that monitors visits to the site, review it regularly and use the information to target your products and messages. Google offers lots of free advice and tips on search engine optimization to help web users find your site.

Asking for Help

Getting your shop in order may require more work than you can do alone. Before you reach the point of overload and burnout is the time to look for help. But this doesn't mean you're suddenly supporting a large payroll. Look for the lowest hanging fruit—usually your family. Has your mom gotten bored with retirement? Perhaps helping you fulfill orders or handle the phone is just what she has been looking for.

Depending on your family dynamics, you may be able to pay a family member for help in ways other than a check. What can you do for your sister if she gives you two afternoons a week? Think about barter and nontraditional payment.

If you do need to hire help, look for people you know and trust, especially as they'll likely be spending time in your home. Your neighborhood or place of worship might have a bulletin board where names are posted. And, of course, there's always word-of-mouth—tell a few good friends you're looking and you just may have what you need.

If you do need help on the cheap, college students can be a wonderful resource. Contact the college or university's job placement office. Sometimes you can get an intern who needs experience for credit, but won't require a salary.

Use caution any time you bring someone into your home-based enterprise, especially if you use sources like job boards or CraigsList.com. Get and check references and arrange for a trial work period to see how things go.

Dealing with Distractions

One friend says the most frequently asked question when people learn she works at home is, "Don't you get distracted by the laundry and other tasks, like snacking?" Yes, there are lots of distractions, as there are at any workplace. It's just that at home there's no one watching over you to make sure you don't succumb to them.

It's not about a particular distraction as much as getting accustomed to a different work environment and managing yourself within it. Certain kinds of distractions may not prevent you from getting your work done, but can impair your professionalism or performance.

For example, if the dog barks every time the FedEx driver pulls up and you're on important calls, something needs to change. If your office is filled with messy distractions like piles of magazines and stacks of bills, you're simply not going to be as efficient as you could be in an orderly space.

Make it work for you. For example, if you're used to a noisy office, you might find yourself working with the TV on. But what if you're having trouble tearing yourself away from the soaps and shows? Try switching to cable news. You'll get the benefit of background noise and the stimulation of keeping up with current events. Turn the sound down every other hour and eventually you'll probably turn it off altogether.

What's hard for many new at-home workers is achieving the right balance. For example, consider a woman who takes her corporate sales job home because she has small children and an aging mother to look after. Because they are such important priorities, she may not see them as distractions. But attending to their non-emergency needs during her designated work hours is no smarter than sneaking out to see what's on sale at your favorite store when you're supposed to be working.

It's all about discipline and boundaries. Here are a few tips from experienced home workers who have done battle with distractions and come out victorious:

Face it. You can't work while you watch your kids. The combination is counterproductive and chaotic. That means you need to work while they're at school or day care or you must bring in someone to watch them—in another part of the house—while you work.

Share the load. Even if you don't belong to a babysitting co-op, seek out neighbors with similar-aged kids. Establish your own child care co-op. Make sure all the adults are equally reliable, especially if you're counting on the time to be out on sales calls when someone else is supposed to be watching your kids.

Find a schedule that works. Without a commute, meetings, breaks, lunch, and pop-in visits from coworkers, you're facing a long day. Some people find themselves overworking. Others find it hard to get motivated without the hustle and bustle of the office. They get distracted by TV, chores, or the Internet and have to steal from family time to make up the work. You now have the luxury of creating your own work flow, breaks, and rewards.

You can always set new goals. Pull out that list of things you planned to do with your newfound time. You may decide to work through lunch and pick the kids up early for a movie or sign up for that pottery course. You've won yourself some breathing room. You can experiment with finding the right balance between working and living on your own terms.

Set and keep boundaries. We know a clothing designer who's worked at home for years. She told a new neighbor, also an at-home worker, to keep her garage door down when she's working. That way, curious friends and neighbors won't see the car and assume it's time to visit. Some people find that they need to establish strict rules at the beginning. For example, no laundry or emptying the dishwasher until after noon. Over time, women who work successfully from home become experts at honoring work hours. They also find that accomplishing housekeeping basics is much easier when you're around the house. Don't be afraid to put a load of laundry in. Just don't let one load evolve into a three-hour laundry and ironing session.

Hang it up. The phone is a huge distraction. As long as your kids' caretakers or schools have your work number, consider not answering your home phone during work time. It's just too tempting.

Clarify the rules. You can't expect your spouse and children to instantly respect your work time and space just because you've declared yourself in business. Think about it—they've been interrupting you for years. One young mom who does medical transcription at home has a good strategy. Because she kept her telephone headset on most of the time, even when she wasn't on a call, the kids couldn't tell if she was on the phone when they'd wander into the office. She established a signal—tapping lightly on her desk—to indicate that she is on a call and can't talk.

If you have school-age kids, welcome them at the door when they come off the bus or from carpool. Get them settled with a snack, then make it clear that until a set time, they're to read or play independently (call it "me time") until you're free to interact again. With a little bit of training, they'll come to enjoy some personal downtime with you nearby.

Engage the family. For some families, having a mom working at home can be a bit confusing. They're used to Mom either full-time at their disposal, or out of the house at a workplace. One way to smooth things out is to get everyone engaged in what you're doing. For example, invite kids eight and older into the office to "work" as your assistant for an hour or two a week. It's amazing how helpful they can be—replenishing office supplies, placing newspapers in the recycling bin, or, if they have their ABCs in order, filing. You may wish to offer a "salary." This can be a couple of dollars to spend on a treat, something experiential like a bike ride with you, or a special certificate you create.

With spouses, it's a little tougher. Many women tell us their husbands want to be part of the process and, when they don't know how, get a little pouty or jealous. First, establish clearly that your spouse wants to be part of your business and then find the logical place. Is your husband a natural promoter? If so, ask him to design and distribute e-flyers announcing your new venture. Is your partner a whiz with figures? Put him or her in charge of the books. Remember to keep communication channels open. Most women are natural communicators, but after a busy or frustrating day you just may want to leave it all behind. Be sure to talk about challenges and successes. Get ideas for new products and new markets. Remember, your name may be on the checks, but it doesn't mean you're in this alone.

Staying Motivated and Responding to Rejections

For most people, working at home means working solo. That is, without the noise and distraction coworkers provide, but also without the natural lift we get when interacting with other people. That means you need to build a support system for yourself. A method for coping with everything from days when you feel a bit blah and unmotivated to stinging disappointments that make you wonder why you became an at-home worker in the first place. In a sense, you have to become your own mentor.

Those who succeed at this say self-talk is a key strategy. Some start every day with a brief, but meaningful pump-up. You can get this from reading a favorite quote about perseverance that you've posted in your office. Or by way of a five-minute meditation session during which you sit quietly, eyes closed, and permit only peaceful, positive thoughts to enter your mind. It may sound silly if you've never indulged in such auto-cheerleading, but it really does help get you in the right frame of mind.

And as all women know, sometimes all it takes is a tiny dose of something positive—an encouraging call or a sincere thank-you—to make us feel more "up." That can change the way we approach our next, or next dozen, sales calls. And it can store up our patience for managing a fussy client or a late delivery.

Here then are a few of our top recommendations for accentuating the positive as you make the transition from their space to yours:

Celebrate small successes. Remember that you're in this for the long haul. If your goal is to find ten new house-sitting clients within six months, recognize incremental progress and reward yourself. Take pride in the steps that get you to the goal, not just the goal itself.

Turn rejection into injection fuel. Think like top athletes and politicians who regularly face disappointment on the field and at the polls. Permit yourself a private moment, or a few, of dejection, then start the climb back up. Look at the situation (a proposal, cold call, or presentation) objectively. Make a list of three things that might have turned things around. Then dig in and find ways to change your offering or your approach. If possible, contact the person who didn't choose you and ask if you might submit or present again next month or next quarter. Get a date on the calendar and work toward nailing the business next time.

Promote yourself. Working at home may mean you no longer have a boss to tell you you've done a great job. And you can't count on clients or colleagues to do that either. Typically, they expect you to perform at the highest level and only have something to say if you fall short. That means sending the atta-girls is up to you. Take time to periodically review your own work and identify what you're doing well and in what ways you've improved. Set specific goals, as a boss would, and monitor your progress toward them. You can even offer yourself a bonus in the form of a massage, a manicure, or a couple hours off for a job well done. You know what motivates you better than anyone else; use that knowledge to your best advantage.

Spread the word. Whether you're planning parties for children or doling out nursing advice on the phone, you need to spread the word. For many of us this is tough, but it can be a great way to stay busy and pumped up through the tough or lean times. Most of us aren't used to tooting our own horns and may never have worked in an environment in which it was necessary. Remember, it's entirely possible to tell your story proudly and convincingly without boasting. This isn't high school, it's the real world of work. Whether you stuff mailboxes with a fun and attractive flyer, send out a plain-vanilla mass e-mail, or spend some time on a personalized phone campaign, let people know what you're up to. It will make you feel better and it will probably bring in work, if not today, then in the near future.

Clear your head. When things get a little crazy, or you've suffered a set-back, give yourself a mental break. For some people this could mean pounding the pavement for a brisk three-mile walk. For someone else it's a matter of getting out of your work space and whipping up a homey dinner for the family. You get the idea—clear the head, get some per-spective, then get back and work your hardest.

You Mean I Get a Coffee Break?

Many people who go out on their own are hard-driving types hell-bent on success. That can mean a fierce focus on work at a high personal cost. But those who have done it successfully insist that all work and no play makes a dull (and potentially miserable) at-home worker.

Rome wasn't built in a day. Your home-based business, no mat-ter how modest, will take some time to get established. Pace your-self and be sure to create ways to stay fresh, focused, and excited.

Build in a coffee break. Do something enjoyable—a few yoga stretches, a brisk ten-minute walk, or read a magazine article. Don't use this time for racing around picking up toys or making your kids' doctors' appoint-ments. Take one (or two) little "time islands" in the day just for you.

Connect with other at-home workers. There are an increasing number of formal and informal ways to do this. Don't be afraid to get together with competitors since it can be a great way to learn and grow. Check with your local chamber of commerce, e-mail message boards, and web-sites to see if these groups exist in your community. If not, create one. Working from home liberates you from hours of daily meetings, but it can also be socially isolating.

Get out of the house. You may not wish to spend the time and money doing this every day, but make occasional lunch dates with friends. Invite a neighbor over for leftovers and conversation. Get out for some exercise several times a week. You'll be amazed at how invigorating it can be to leave the office, albeit briefly, especially if you're baking cupcakes, tutoring online, or fulfilling other solo pursuits.

ACTION STEPS: *Setting Up Shop*

Creating the physical and emotional space you need to work from home is one of the most exciting parts of the process. Consider these action steps to help you do it better:

1. *Audit your house.* Of course, you know the place like the back of your hand, but think creatively about where and how to carve out working space. Is your mom or best girlfriend better than you at this kind of thing? Enlist her help to figure out where you might work. Run the ideas by your family. Although you probably don't need permission, you will score points by reviewing your plan with everyone.

2. *Create and stick to a budget.* Figure out how much you have to spend on setting up shop and don't spend more. If that means going for used rather than new furniture, so be it. Spending more than you want, or have, isn't a good way to start off.

3. *Get what's coming to you.* If you're taking your old job home, or hooking up with a company that's hiring you to work from home, make sure you get what's due. That could mean anything from a computer and travel expenses to health insurance. Some companies may not be forthcoming unless you ask.

4. *Do your tax tasks.* Using a portion of your home for business purposes may mean new tax deductions for you. Even if you do your own taxes, a couple of hours with a CPA can be a wise investment. Find out what percentage of home expenses (including mortgage or rent, heat and air-conditioning, maintenance) you can legally deduct, and what kind of records you must keep. Start now so the habit will form.

5. *Look the part.* Once you've announced you're going home, you'll want to look like a success even if you aren't yet one. That does not mean wearing a suit and panty hose, but be sure to get dressed, even casually, every morning. Don't shuffle around the house, showerless and in slippers. You're working—feeling and looking successful is important.

chapter ten

■ ■ ■

Home Economics

You're on the path home—as a teleworking employee, an independent contractor, a direct sales representative, or a soon-to-be new business owner. Congratulations! You've taken an important step in taking control of your life.

But with control comes new responsibilities. Now that you're the boss in your new workplace, you're also the chief financial officer, legal manager, bookkeeper, and tax expert for your new venture.

Don't panic! Even if you were never good at math and your legal expertise comes from watching *Law and Order*, you can do this. Others have successfully navigated through the legal and accounting tangles of the small-business world.

What You Don't Know
Can Hurt You

The important thing is to ask questions. Successful entrepreneurs know how to ask for advice and when to seek professional help. They learn to take advantage of the many free resources available to help them turn their dreams into money-making enterprises. You can, too.

You say you're a whiz at making gift baskets or creating websites or you have the dynamic personality and drive to sell beauty products, but know nothing about business licenses or liability insurance? It's time to learn. Accounting may sound boring and taxes scary, but you need to know how to keep yourself and your business safe, legal, and profitable. The things we're going to be talking about are the nuts and bolts for your financial success. And you want to make money, right?

With a positive attitude and a step-by-step approach, you'll find these issues are quite manageable. A little research, organizing, and planning will get you past the setting-up-shop hurdles and on to

Home Helper

American Express surveyed small-business owners to see where they go for advice. The most popular responses were individual mentors, social networks, trade associations, business advisors, the Internet, and chambers of commerce. Before you start working from home or launch your new business, think about your own network of professional friends. Buy a Rolodex or make a list of those you can call on to answer your questions. Keep it at your fingertips. There's no reason to reinvent the wheel when you can borrow from those who have faced and met similar challenges.

the fun part of working from home—selling your crafts, designing your logos, and being your own boss.

We can't hope to cover everything on the legal, accounting, and tax front in one chapter, but we will alert you to important topics you need to consider and questions you'll need to answer in order to start working from home with confidence. Attending to financial and legal issues up front will save you time, money, and trouble down the path.

Know Your Resources

Were you employed for years and finally decided to go out on your own as a consultant or independent contractor? Perhaps you're switching fields or starting a freelance career. This may be your first job or your first company. No one expects you to know the ropes of being self-employed. Fortunately, others have written excellent guides for the trail. Check out these resources:

- The Small Business Administration (SBA.gov), a government agency founded to aid, counsel, assist, and protect the interests of small businesses in the U.S., is one of the best resources for entrepreneurs. You'll find a vast array of free and low-cost courses, seminars, online training, publications, individual counseling, and loan guarantee programs to help you start and grow your company. Visit the site to find a local office and resources.

- Check out Women's Business Centers sponsored by the SBA. Each state has one to help women get started in business. See the SBA website.

- SCORE, the Service Corps of Retired Executives (SCORE.org, 800-634-0245) harnesses the power of more than 10,000

retired and working executives who volunteer their time to provide one-on-one business mentoring and coaching. SCORE has
nearly 400 locations and offers online coaching. Its services are
free and confidential.

- The Internal Revenue Service (IRS.gov). The IRS can be your new
best friend as you start your business. They're savvy about business
operations and challenges and share their knowledge through their
website, online learning courses, publications, and over the phone.
Their publications can answer a lot of your questions.

- Your local chamber of commerce is a great place to network and
learn more about your community. Many chambers have small-
business committees where you can meet other entrepreneurs
and discuss common problems and solutions. The chamber
may also be the place to find regulatory advice, vendors, marketing services, and new customers.

- Many colleges have continuing education departments that
offer courses on entrepreneurship, e-commerce, bookkeeping,
and other small business and self-employed topics of interest.
Most programs are affordable and at convenient hours (nights
and weekends). Some colleges also have microbusiness development centers within their business departments.

- State departments of labor often have career centers or economic development offices to help people manage their voca-
tions. Learn what resources are available in your state.

- Trade or professional associations let you meet others involved
in your field. The members will understand questions and
issues specific to your industry. This is a good place to ask for
referrals to other professionals who are familiar with your busi-

ness and have helped others—lawyers, accountants, bookkeep-
ers, public relations firms. You may even find a mentor.

- Don't overlook people who are already successful at what you
  want to do. Search for someone in a different city or state and
  ask if they'd be willing to serve as an advisor to your start-up.
  People are often generous in this way. An Atlanta woman who
  wanted to open an eldercare agency contacted the owner of a
  similar company in an adjacent state. Because their goals were
  similar, but their markets different, the established owner took
  the newcomer under her wing. Another good place to find
  mentors is through the SBA Women's Network for Entrepreneurial Training (SBA.gov).

Get and Stay Organized

Record-keeping is much easier if you're well-organized. Allbusi
ness.com has some good ideas for setting up a home office. Buy a
file cabinet and folders and keep all work-related papers in one
place. Set up files for your business plan, budget, licenses, insurance,
and other necessary items. Save receipts for everything you buy to
work from home, including this guide. Start thinking about how
you will invoice for your services, record income, and keep track of
expenses and inventory. Buy the equipment and supplies you need.

Everyone's files will differ. A writer needs files for article ideas
and query letters sent to magazines, as well as a log of projects she's
working on. A personal trainer may want a file of health and fitness
information and letters from satisfied clients he can use for references. One woman we knew had a "Lord only knows" file for
important items that didn't yet fit a category. You laugh, but she
never lost anything. Expect your files to grow with your business.

Don't forget organizational aides like a calendar, day-planner book, Rolodex, or business card holder for your growing network of experts and customers. Many managers keep a "tickler file" in an accordion folder with the dates of the month at the top. Use it to remind you to complete applications, call clients, set up meetings, or pay bills on time. Simply check the contents each day and attend to it.

 ## Home Helper

A small notebook can be your best low-budget organizational tool. Every evening or morning write your business and personal to-do list in it. As you complete tasks, cross them off. The real trick is learning to prioritize. You can cross a lot of small things off your list in a hurry, but still not accomplish the big things that will move your business forward. Put a star by the real-difference makers, or list them at the top as a must-do list.

Break intimidating tasks into smaller parts. You want to hire an accountant but are afraid of making a mistake and wasting money. List the steps, such as: call mentor or colleague for recommendation; make a list of what you want the accountant to do; write a list of interview questions that will help you judge the effectiveness of prospective candidates; interview several accountants, asking for references and fees; call references; hire an accountant. These tasks may stretch over a number of days, but as you cross each one off, you are nearer your goal.

For worriers there's a great benefit to writing out tomorrow's to-do list at the end of today. Once that swarm of tasks is written down, your subconscious can rest. You can enjoy your leisure time and sleep better.

Records as Business Tools

People use a variety of record-keeping systems, both handwritten and computer-based. The important thing is that the system be efficient and understandable to you and anyone you hire to help you manage your accounts or taxes. No matter what systems you use, decide to establish and maintain good records from the outset. Good records will:

- Reveal how your business is doing. You'll be able to see at a glance when added expenses are cutting into your profits, when you have too much inventory, or what products are selling better than others. The numbers will tell you where your business is growing and where it's in trouble. By making it a habit to maintain and update your books at least monthly, you'll be able to make adjustments to operations as you go along to increase your profitability.

- Help you prepare financial statements, such as profit-and-loss and balance sheets that will help you manage your business. If you need to apply for a business loan or credit, investors will want to see your financial statements in order to assess their own risk.

- Keep accurate track of deductible expenses. Every deductible dollar missed (because you lost the receipt or failed to write it down) increases your taxes, and decreases your profit.

- Make it much easier to file your tax returns. You want to be able to prove to the IRS that you're a business, not a hobby. In the case of an audit, you're going to need written proof to show that your returns are accurate.

- Give you greater peace of mind. There's a lot to keep track of when running a business. Staying organized helps you not to miss important tax or loan deadlines, product trends, or new opportunities.

Home Helper

The National Society of Accountants (NSA) (nsacct.org) advises home-based businesses "to file important records immediately. Resist any tendency to set aside important records for filing later. These include copies of client checks, accounting records, legal documents, tax documents, insurance records, expense reports, and more. Once you start down the road to delaying filing, the problem only gets worse, and eventually you may lose something important. Take five minutes to file documents when you deal with them so you don't have to worry about it later."

Choosing a Business Structure

Businesses are organized in different ways for various reasons. You may need a lawyer or accountant to help you choose the best structure for your needs. Some common types of business organization and their benefits and drawbacks include:

Sole Proprietorship

This is the simplest and least expensive form of business entity and the choice of many self-employed workers and independent contractors. You'll need appropriate business licenses and a sales tax permit if you are selling goods. You'll report the profits and losses of your business on your personal income tax return by using Schedule

C or C-EZ. You can write off legitimate business expenses and take advantage of tax-sheltered retirement plans. The downside is that there is no separation between you and the business. You are personally liable for business debts or lawsuits, and if you should need a loan, creditors will be looking over your personal credit status.

Partnership

When two or more people decide to go into business together, sharing responsibilities, profits, and losses, they can form a partnership. They each report their share of the profits on their personal tax returns. You'll want to write a partnership agreement to define duties, determine how decisions will be made, and how profits and losses are to be divided. See IRS Publication 541 to see how to form a partnership and Form 1065 to see what a partnership tax return looks like. In a general partnership, all partners are liable for all business debts and court judgments. Personal assets are at risk. In a limited partnership, limited partners don't participate in management and have limited personal liability for business debts.

Limited Liability Company/Partnership (LLC)

This is a relatively new and increasingly popular form of business organization allowed by state statute according to the IRS. It's less complicated to set up than a corporation, yet owners reap the same benefits of limited personal liability for the debts and actions of the LLC. No stock is issued. It also provides for management flexibility and the benefit of pass-through taxation. (The LLC pays no tax. Members file their profits and losses on their individual tax returns.) IRS Publication 3402 can help you decide if this structure is right for you.

Corporation (Inc., Ltd.)

Organized through the authority of a state government, the corporation is a complex business structure with more start-up costs. It is a separate legal entity with its own tax-reporting requirements. It owns its own assets and is responsible for corporate debts. Owners must issue stock certificates to themselves, hold annual meetings, and elect directors. Profits are taxed at the corporate level and again when distributed to shareholders, but owners have limited personal

Home Helper

There are many good reasons for hiring a professional accountant before the business starts, according to the National Society of Accountants (NSA). "First, what kind of entity should be chosen for the business operation? This is not a one-size-fits-all decision, as there are more than thirty factors to be considered in choosing what entity the business will be. One of the major factors to consider is the potential liabilities related to the business. If the business operation will result in added liability potential for the owner, the entity choice should be one that will help shield the owner's personal assets. Another major factor is the need for fringe benefits, such as health insurance and medical reimbursement plans. These fringe benefits have tax-favored status in some entities, but not others. Also, some entities result in a higher administrative burden for the business, and some owners are more capable than others to deal with the higher administrative load. The accountant is often the professional who does most of the paperwork for a start-up business, and uses a checklist to be sure that all requirements are met. You can find a qualified accountant in your area: Visit nsacct.org and click 'Find a Professional.'"

liability for business debt. If the corporation qualifies as an S Corporation with the IRS, then owners can avoid double taxation. Profits flow through to shareholders who report it on their personal tax returns. There are do-it-yourself guidelines to help people incorporate, but most people hire an attorney. A small business may start out as a sole proprietor or partnership and decide to incorporate later as the business grows.

You'll want to consider the costs, personal liability, company financing, tax benefits, and size of your company when deciding on a business structure. To change a business entity, owners must fill out IRS Form 8832, Entity Classification Election.

You May Need an EIN

If you have employees, organize your business as a corporation or partnership, have a Keogh plan, or file tax returns for employment, excise, alcohol, tobacco, or firearms, you will need to apply for an Employer Identification Number (also known as a Federal Tax Identification number). Think of it as a Social Security number for your business. Use it to open a business bank account, apply for licenses, and file tax returns. You don't need one if you're a sole proprietor with no employees, but to protect your identity you may want to invoice using an EIN rather than your Social Security number.

You can find out if you need an EIN, apply, and receive an EIN online, but it will take two weeks before the EIN becomes part of the IRS's permanent records. You can also apply over the phone (800-829-4933) or fax Form SS-4 to your state IRS service center. You should have an EIN before making a first tax return or quarterly payment for your business.

Licenses, Permits, and
Other Legalities

Most municipalities and counties require businesses to hold a business license. Certain occupations require a state license or certification to operate (such as beauticians, private investigators, realtors, building contractors). Ask your chamber of commerce or Small Business Administration office which licenses you'll need, then contact the appropriate government offices directly. Fill out the applications and pay the fee. You'll probably have to renew each year.

Those selling merchandise to customers will need a sales tax license or permit to be able to collect sales tax. Contact your state's department of revenue or franchise tax board for an application.

Some businesses require permits to operate legally. If your business is retail, you may need a seller's permit. If you're serving or selling food, you'll need a health permit. Remodeling your home office or garage requires a building permit. Permits generally come with regulations and inspections. See why you bought that file cabinet?

Zoning Matters

Before you move your business into your home, make sure it's legal to operate a business there. Some residential zoning ordinances exclude home-based businesses, while others allow a home "occupation," as long as the home is used primarily as a residence. Some apartment complexes and condominium boards have rules against home-based businesses. Residential communities fear extra traffic, parking issues, noise, unsightly signs, or commercial deliveries.

Read your zoning ordinance carefully before launching your business. If businesses aren't allowed, you may be able to apply for a variance through the local zoning board. Your request is more likely to be approved if you can show that your business has minimal impact on your neighbors and the community.

Worker Status

If you'll be hiring your services out to employers or hiring employees for your own business, one of the things you'll need to know is the legal (and tax) differences between an independent contractor and employee. Be sure to read IRS Publication 1779. Two cate-

🏠 Home Helper

The National Society of Accountants notes "that the IRS has specific criteria to determine whether people working for a business are independent contractors or employees. This is a very troublesome issue for a lot of new businesses. Many small business owners think they cannot afford to pay the required payroll taxes, unemployment taxes, workers compensation insurance, etc., for their workers. But this kind of thinking can have disastrous consequences. Even worse than the substantial tax penalties is the catastrophic result of having a worker who is hurt on the job with no insurance coverage. The truth is small business owners cannot afford to treat a worker who is a legitimate employee as anything but an employee. If there is any doubt, the employer should stay on the safe side. By paying payroll taxes and filing payroll tax returns, a statute of limitations is established and non-filing penalties are eliminated. This substantially reduces the penalties for misclassification if a worker is later determined to be misclassified. Criteria exist to determine if people are self-employed or independent contractors—to access complete IRS information on this topic, visit irs.gov and type 'Independent Contractor' into the search field."

gories of employees that are treated as nonemployees for federal employment tax purposes are real estate salespersons and direct sellers of consumer goods. They're considered independent contractors because they work on commission.

Hobby vs. Business

Another misclassification you'll want to avoid is having your business be classified as a hobby by the IRS. You're a great cook and occasionally cater parties for your friends, but you keep buying expensive kitchen equipment to do it. Is your activity a business or a hobby? If your catering business isn't incorporated and loses money year after year, you could be in danger of having the IRS classify your hard work as a hobby. If this happens, you lose valuable business deductions. You can't use your losses to offset other income or carry them to the next year. End result—you'll owe more income tax.

The difference between a hobby and a business in the eyes of the IRS is whether you have a profit motive. How do you prove that your intentions are monetary, and you're not just indulging your passion and writing off the expenses?

- Earn a profit (even a small one counts) for three out of five consecutive years. You may want to put off buying new equipment until after January 1, if it means the difference between a profit and a loss.

- Operate in a businesslike manner: Have a business license, open a business bank account, print business cards and letterhead, install a business phone, and join the chamber of commerce.

- Keep a log of your business activity, contacts made, letters sent to clients—anything that would show you are trying to earn a profit.

- If you don't earn a profit in three out of five years, you may still be able to convince the IRS that you are running a business, but it will be harder.

Accounting Matters

Yes it does! No matter how much you love the idea of working from home or designing a business around your passion, you want the impact on your budget to be positive. Start-up ventures often cost more and take longer to get off the ground than you would expect. So before making the transition, get your personal finances in order.

Balance your family budget. Pay off debts and eliminate unnecessary purchases before giving up your steady paycheck. Check your personal credit rating through Equifax, Experian, or Trans-Union, and clean up any errors. Since you don't have a business credit history, lenders will look at your personal finances if you need a loan or line of credit to buy supplies or equipment.

"Establish a realistic budget [for your business] to include income, projection, and costs of doing business—i.e., phones, supplies, advertising, and business meals," says Karla K. Dennis, president of Cohesive, a professional tax firm in California that offers a complete tax and accounting service to individuals and businesses. "Monthly, review your budget to actual numbers and determine what needs to be done to improve your numbers. Do not allow your review to go past thirty days. This will cost you time and money."

⊞ Home Helper

Look for ways to save money, such as bundling your phone, computer, and cable services. Buy everyday supplies, such as copier paper and printer ink on sale and in large quantities. Check the phone book or Internet for used office furniture stores in your area. Did you know that you could find low-cost business services through Costco? Visit costco.com and click on Services.

As expenses start adding up, you may be tempted to scrimp. Do you really need a second phone line? Yes, it's part of your professional image. Do you really want your teenager greeting customers with "Yo, whazzup?" Purchase what you need to efficiently operate from home.

"Anticipate your equipment needs for a copier, scanner, and printer as if you were at the peak of your business. To obtain a huge account and not be able to service it would not sit well. Be self-contained and able to run your business internally. This will cost you less and prevent you from making midnight runs to a business service center," says Dennis.

Separate Business and Personal Finances

Whether your work is part-time or full-time, open a business checking account, preferably one with an ATM debit/credit card attached. Choose a bank that you trust with a full line of business services. Banking online can save you time.

Deposit business income and pay for business expenses with your business account. This will make it easier to track your business activity for record-keeping purposes and streamline your tax filing. Transfer money to your personal account when you need it. Not only is a business account a wise accounting move, but psychologically, it helps to keep your business and personal hats separate.

⊞ Home Helper

Make it a habit to pay all business bills by check and write in the purchase item, so that you'll have added proof of deductions at tax time. When you receive checks from clients, write "for deposit only," on the back and put them in the bank as soon as possible. Balance your checkbook every month.

Update Your Books Often

An effective bookkeeping system is essential for your financial health. If you haven't a clue about keeping records, learn the basics. Take a class at your community college or through the SBA. Get online help through SCORE or the allbusiness.com Finance and Accounting center. An excellent source of information is IRS Publication 583, "Starting a Business and Keeping Records." Even if you hire an accountant to help you choose and maintain a system, you still need to understand it.

Good communication is critical between you and all the professionals you work with—the more they understand your business, the more they can help. If you use the same computer accounting system as your accountant it will make it easier to transfer information at tax time. However, many self-employed people keep their own books and do their own taxes in the beginning.

Most small businesses today use computerized bookkeeping systems, such as Intuit's *QuickBooks* or Peachtree's *Peachtree Accounting*, but many self-employed workers use ledger pads and calculators. You might also find *Quicken* and *Microsoft Money* to be useful programs.

 Home Helper

Software or shoeboxes? According to the National Society of Accountants, "It is imperative for a business to keep accurate records, but the bookkeeping method is not as critical as the end result. An owner with computer skills will probably wish to set up a computerized system and many accountants will help the owner choose software and set up an appropriate system. However, a series of envelopes categorized and stored in a shoebox can be an accurate record-keeping system for a small business. The important thing is that the owner understands and maintains the records! An accountant can also explain the special records required for automobile use, business meals, entertainment, and business use of the home, so that tax deductions will not be missed due to sloppy records."

When setting up records, keep these things in mind:

- You have to choose a cash- or accrual-based method of accounting. Check the IRS for definitions. What you choose will depend on the size and type of your business. According to the NSA, "Both methods have pros and cons. It's easier to make the right choice in the beginning. Changing accounting methods requires a long, difficult form (IRS Form 3115) that carries an IRS user fee. Consult your accountant for the best option."

- Sales tax, if applicable. Don't forget to deduct sales tax from the recording of your retail sales figures.

- Auto expenses. If you drive your car for business, you can deduct auto expenses. The IRS offers two methods. You can take actual expenses, such as gas, oil, lease fees, repairs, licenses, and depreciation for the percentage that you use your car for business. Or you can take a standard mileage rate (50.5 cents per mile) for the number of business miles you log. If you want to take mileage, you have to start from the first year you start using a car for business purposes. Tracking mileage is easier—you just keep a mileage log in your car and record date, business purpose, and odometer readings at the beginning and end of each trip—but it may not give you the largest deduction. Consult your accountant. Office supply stores have mileage logs. Remember, when you work from home all miles to visit clients, apply for licenses, do research, pick up supplies, etc., are considered business miles. The IRS also allows mileage deductions for charity work and trips for medical needs. You can use one log for all your mileage purposes.

- Keep an asset journal on all equipment that you purchase for your business, such as computers, cell phones, copiers, or office furniture. Record date of purchase, price, and purpose. You will need this information to take either a Section 179 deduction or depreciate the asset for a deduction on your tax return.

- Your record-keeping gets more complicated when you hire employees, as you add payroll, federal and state income tax withholding, federal unemployment taxes, workers' compensation insurance, and the paperwork for any fringe benefits you offer. The Small Business Administration can help you sort through the paperwork.

- If you are selling a product, set up a credit card payment system for your customers. You can set up a merchant credit card processing system or use PayPal (PayPal.com), a secure system used for eBay transactions among others. Consider the cost and convenience of various systems.

- Save records. Generally, the IRS says you must save tax records until the period of limitations for a tax return runs out. This means the period in which you can amend your tax return or the IRS can assess additional tax. It ranges from three to six years, but is indefinite if you've filed a fraudulent return. Keep employment records at least four years. To be on the safe side, SCORE recommends keeping all tax records for at least seven years.

- Reconcile your books with your bank statement each month. It's also good to total expenses and income each month to measure profitability.

- Create a backup. Print out copies of computer-based files. Copy written records as well. Store copies in a separate location than originals. Computers crash. The NSA advises small-business owners to back up their data every night. "How much is a day's work on the computer worth to you? Probably a lot! Make sure you have an external computer backup of your critical computer-based intellectual property and records each night. You can do it yourself with an external hard drive, or a service can back it up to another location via the Internet each night. Having data stored on a server outside the home also protects you in the event of theft, fire, flood, or other disaster."

- Transfer your business knowledge to a trusted person, suggests the NSA. "In many home-based businesses, the owner is the chief cook and bottle washer and critical data about the company is contained in his or her head. Protect your business by sharing important knowledge about the business structure, client base, vendors, banks, and other information with a trusted person, whether it's a spouse, business colleague, accountant, or lawyer. If something happens to you, it will be much easier for them to pick up the pieces."

- When destroying old records, shred them.

 Home Helper

Proper and timely billing is important to the success of your work. An invoice should always include:

- Your business name, address, and EIN

- An invoice number—you can assign them numerically by year, such as 09001, 09002, 09003, etc.

- Date

- Customer name and address

- Description of goods or services

- Amount due

- Terms, such as "Paid in Full 30 days"

- Expenses, if client agreed to pay them. For figuring mileage, use the rate set by the client

- Copies of receipts for expenses, if required

Insurance Issues

Benefits are what you most likely will miss the most if you're moving from employee to self-employed status. Health and other insurance is about to come solely out of your pocket now. To make matters worse, the monthly premiums and copayments will probably be higher and the coverage may be less comprehensive. The good news is that your insurance premiums should be tax deductible. Shop around to find the best deals and make an informed decision. Expect this to take a couple of months. Here are some of the kinds of insurance you'll need to consider:

Health

Health insurance premiums have been rising annually at double-digit rates for companies—don't expect it to be any better for individuals. As one SCORE advisor put it, "The term affordable health insurance is an oxymoron."

If you are leaving a company that offered group health coverage, your best bet is to sign up for COBRA (COBRAInsurance.com). The Consolidated Omnibus Budget Reconciliation Act is a federal law that will allow you to keep your employer's health plan for eighteen months. The rates will no longer be subsidized by your company, so your monthly premiums will be higher, but probably less than individual coverage. It will give you time to shop for another plan.

Health insurance is regulated at the state level and the availability and cost depend on factors like your age, gender, weight, health history, and location. You can compare and contrast policies on the Internet at Insure.com or eHealthInsurance.com, or work with an insurance agent or broker. Choose an agent who represents a variety of companies and can tell you the advantages and disadvantages

⊞ Home Helper

Reading insurance coverage information is tedious and confusing. Before you begin to compare policies, make a list of what you want your policy to cover, such as hospital stays, surgery, doctor visits, diagnostic tests, prescriptions, rehabilitation therapy, etc. If you're of childbearing age, make sure the policies cover prenatal and birth costs. Not all policies do. Check copays and premium costs. You can make sure your health insurance company has a good reputation and rating at Best's Insurance Reports (AMBest.com) or Duff & Phelps (DuffandPhelps.com).

of each. Beware of anyone who has a one-size-fits-all solution. Ask for agent recommendations from people you trust.

Want to save money? Find a group plan! Most states will let businesses with as few as two employees buy a group plan. It pays to ask. You can also join a trade association for your industry or a professional organization that offers group insurance coverage. You'll have to pay membership dues, but these are tax deductible.

Here are some possible sources:

- If your job is connected with the media in any way—try Media-Bistro's AvantGuild for dental, health, life, and disability insurance (MediaBistro.com).

- Self-employed? The National Association for the Self-Employed (NASE.org) gives members access to benefits and business advice.

- Check out the Freelancers Union for jobs and insurance (Free lancersunion.org).

- Are you in contracting or building design? Home Depot Business ToolBox offers group insurance and other benefits. See HDBusinessToolBox.com.

- Costco members can find more than groceries at this discounter. Visit Costco.com and click on services to find a full range of individual and small-business services, including auto and home insurance, group dental, small-business 401(k), home-equity financing, and payroll services.

- Check your chamber of commerce to see if they have a group insurance plan for their small-business members.

Home Business

You probably already have home insurance, but that policy was not meant to cover a home-based business. For instance, the cost of your brand-new computer and other equipment may not be fully covered under your home furnishings. Suppose the basement floods and drowns your inventory? What if your laptop is stolen on a business trip? A home policy will generally cover accidents to visitors in your residence, but will it cover clients? It's best to talk to your home insurance agent and add appropriate riders to your home policy rather than risk a lawsuit. You may also find an in-home business policy, which may come with liability insurance.

Disability

You love the work you do, but what if you become ill and can't work? Disability insurance can help you and your family to make it through a period when you're without income due to an accident or illness.

⊞ Home Helper

According to the NSA, "Most employees of large companies automatically receive short-term and long-term disability insurance as part of a benefits package. It's easy to forget about this in a home-business environment, yet the risk of becoming disabled remains the same. Look into disability insurance plans and choose one that matches your financial needs. Often, the best disability plan at the most reasonable cost is one that you obtain through the group plan of a professional association."

Liability

This helps protect you and your business from lawsuits caused by accidents that happen in your workplace or with your products. Do you really need it? Unless you never have contact with vendors, clients, suppliers, the UPS man, or customers in your home office—yes, you probably do. Consider these scenarios:

- A vendor slips on water on your front walk and breaks an ankle while delivering your supplies.

- A customer has an allergic reaction to an ingredient in your homemade candy and has to be hospitalized.

- One of the children you keep in your day-care business hits another with a toy truck. The gash needs stitches.

- While pressing a customer's expensive gown that you've just altered, as part of your alterations business, you burn a hole in it.

- Inventory stacked in your basement topples over and injures your child's playmate.

- An employee driving the company van accidentally hits a pedestrian.

Accidents happen and in today's litigious society people sue over almost anything, so it's best to be prepared. How much liability insurance you need will depend on the size and type of your business, and the amount of risk involved. Get several opinions from insurers and compare policies and prices.

Errors and Omissions (E & O)

This is a specific liability insurance that protects against negligence or unintentional errors and omissions in your line of work. For instance, your printing company accidentally prints the wrong phone number for an event poster and the error isn't caught until after the posters have been distributed. E & O insurance would help pay legal fees and the settlement if the client sued and you were found to be at fault. Consultants and service providers of all kinds benefit from E & O insurance.

Automobile and Truck

Obviously, any vehicle you use for business needs to have coverage, even your personal car that you use for business purposes. If you're planning to add significant driving miles for your business, drive clients frequently, or deliver goods—let your insurance agent know. There is tremendous competition among auto insurers, so shop around.

Workers' Compensation

You are required by your state to provide death and disability insurance for your employees should they get hurt on the job. Some states have a plan they offer to employers, which may be more cost-effective than a private policy.

Home Helper

To save money on insurance, opt for the highest deductibles you can afford and ask about discounts for having several different types of insurance with one company.

Taxing Matters

As a self-employed worker, you've said good-bye to corporate W-2s and short tax forms. The checks you get from clients or customers will have no income tax deducted. Furthermore, you'll be responsible for paying your full share of self-employment taxes (Social Security and Medicare), not just half, as when you worked. You'll have to determine what you owe the federal, state, and local governments. This is when those accurate records you've been keeping will pay dividends.

As a self-employed worker, you'll need to pay income tax, self-employment tax, and estimated taxes unless you earn very little from your business. A good rule of thumb is to save a third of every check you receive to pay taxes. You may owe a little more or considerably less depending on what other income or deductions you have, but in any case, saving a third of your income should eliminate a bill that you can't afford to pay on April 15.

The forms you file will depend on your business organization and the types of deductions you take. Check with the IRS, and click on the "Small Business and Self-Employed One-Stop Resource." The way to save money on taxes is to know and take all of the business deductions you are allowed.

As a sole proprietor, you'll be filing a Schedule C with your 1040, and a Schedule SE to figure your self-employment tax, whether you're filing alone, married, or as head of your household. Here are some of the Schedule C (Profit or Loss From Business) deductions you may be eligible to take:

- Money you spent on advertising your business.

- Car and truck expenses, either the actual-expense method or the standard mileage deduction.

- Depreciation and amortization of office equipment you buy. You may choose to take the entire cost the first year, or depreciate the property over a number of years. The IRS dictates how many years for different types of equipment.

- Legal and professional services. You can deduct the fees of your lawyer or accountant.

- Insurance, other than health.

- Office expenses. This include supplies, business stationery, postage, photocopies, telephone expenses, etc.

- Rent or lease of vehicles, machinery, or equipment.

- Repairs and maintenance to machinery.

- Taxes and licenses.

- Travel for business and half the cost of meals and entertainment for clients.

- Other. This might include conferences, professional dues, subscriptions to trade magazines, etc.

Estimated Taxes

Employees have taxes taken out of every paycheck—a pay-as-you-go plan. When you're self-employed, the government expects you to pay your tax bill quarterly if you expect to owe more than $1000 in federal tax at the end of the year. Write these dates on your calendar now—April 15, June 15, September 15, and January 15, and be prepared to mail in a 1040-ES with your estimated tax before those dates. To avoid penalties, you need to pay at least 90 percent of what you owe annually, or 100 percent of the tax you paid the previous year.

You can figure your estimated taxes for the next year when you file your annual taxes—simply take the tax you owed and divide by four. When your income goes up, increase your estimated taxes accordingly to save a high tax bill at the end of the year. To learn more, see IRS Publication 505, "Tax Withholding and Estimated Tax."

Home-Office Deduction

One of the great advantages of working at home is the home office deduction—if you qualify. Read IRS Publication 587, "Business Use of Your Home." To qualify, the IRS says that your home office must be used exclusively (no sharing the office with a guest room, for example) and regularly for business and that it must be your principal place of business. The deduction is limited to the amount of business income. To calculate what percentage of your home, apartment, or condo you use for business, you may either count the number of rooms (if they are of about equal size) and divide by the total number of rooms in your home to get a percentage, or you can measure the square footage of your office and divide by the total square footage of your home. Some of the related deductions you may be eligible to take include the business percentage of your mortgage interest, rent, insurance, real estate tax, utilities, repairs, and home depreciation.

⊞ Home Helper

"IRS audits look closely at any space in your home that you claim as a home office," according to the NSA. They suggest that you "take photos of your home office, measure the space, and draw a simple diagram showing its square footage in relation to the entire home. Make sure that everything in the office is business-related—no toys on the floor, etc. Better yet, if you have an architect's drawing of your home, copy it and highlight the areas used for business. If you also use a shed or garage, do the same documentation for them. Keep these documents in a permanent file for tax purposes."

Retirement Planning

Like record-keeping, buying insurance, and paying taxes, setting up a retirement account for your new job or business is all up to you. Fortunately, there are two very good reasons to open a retirement account. 1) You are making your future much more secure financially. You don't plan to work forever, and 2) You're reducing the amount of taxes you will owe. Even better news, many of the plans are easy to set up and in some cases you can contribute more than you can to a normal individual retirement plan. Ask your accountant about a SEP-IRA, Roth IRA, or Keogh plan, and read IRS Publication 560, "Retirement Plans for Small Business."

Home Helper

The NSA notes that "home-based business owners usually don't have access to 401(k) plans and other retirement savings options available at large companies. As of 2007, the annual $4,000 deduction most taxpayers can take for IRA contributions ($5,000 for those fifty or older) is fine, but you can usually put away much more through a SEP-IRA. [The IRS says up to about 20 percent of your net income!] But be careful—if you contribute to your regular IRA you may not be eligible for larger SEP-IRA contribution deductions in the same year. Consult an accountant for details."

Taking Care of Business

There are a great number of financial and legal details to consider when you decide to work from home. Taking the time now to lay a good foundation—to set up good record-keeping systems, insure against risks, and know what to expect when taxes come due—will bring rich rewards. You'll make every penny of your new income count. You'll feel confident about your business sense, and you'll have more time and energy to put into the work you want to do.

Resources

- Small Business Administration: SBA.gov
- Counselors to small business, SCORE: SCORE.org
- Internal Revenue Service: IRS.gov
- National Society of Accountants: NSACCT.org

- Legal information: Nolo.com

- Insurance: Insure.com

- eHealth Insurance Services, Inc.: eHealthInsurance.com

- Business Advice: AllBusiness.com

- National Association for Self-Employed: NASE.org

- National Federation of Independent Business: NFIB.org

ACTION STEPS: *Home Economics*

1. *Buy a calendar book strictly for transition purposes.* Decide when you want to be up and running at home—three months, six months? Write the specific tasks you'll need to complete (from your business plan) on specific dates that will let you meet that goal.

2. *Find three other people who work from home doing work similar to what you want to do.* Invite each one for lunch and an informational interview. Ask them to tell you their stories. What do they like about their jobs and lifestyles? What were their biggest obstacles? Their greatest successes? Get their best legal, organizational, financial, and tax advice. Take notes. Ask for resources, and if you can call them when you have more specific questions.

3. *Buy a file cabinet (even a crate will do) and start setting up a business research file based on some of the topics we've covered.* As you find good information, file it under the appropriate topic. You may not need it now, but chances are you will later.

4. *Save all receipts and record all home-business–related expenses.*

5. *Type up and print out the above resources, and make sure to check off each as you contact them for key needs.*

chapter eleven

■ ■ ■

Now It's Up to You

You've thought about it. You may even have fantasized about it—a life with no commute, no dress code, and no limits. The freedom to determine your own work style and to respond to the shifting priorities that life brings your way. For you, and a growing number of people, working at home makes an awful lot of sense.

That includes people raising young children or assisting aging parents. It encompasses those with an untapped entrepreneurial spirit finally permitted to soar. It embraces those who refuse to commute scores of miles each day, burning fossil fuels *and* burning the candle at both ends. And it also includes those who have helped their bosses to realize that taking their current jobs home can be a win-win.

Whether you have a medical challenge that makes home preferable or simply have had enough with panty hose and constant meetings, we applaud you and your decision.

It's Going to Take Some Work

We know, because we've done it, that really making this work takes much more than wanting it to work. The fact that you've gotten through at least one book on the subject says a lot about your motivation. Now use what you've learned, including the results of the exercises and action steps in each chapter. Take advantage of the resources section that follows. Consider going back through the book quickly with a highlighter or a pad of sticky notes to flag sections you want to use or return to.

Focus on the End

Once you've done the reading, reflecting, and reaching out, start to focus on an end result. Although there's no certainty it will be the right one, asking questions like those that follow will make it more likely that you're heading in a good direction.

- Is the end result in keeping with your passion, interests, and abilities?

- Are you prepared for the potential uncertainty, looser schedule, and 24/7 demands that working at home can impose?

- Does your direction reflect market realities and best indications about future trends?

- If your intent is to take your current job home, have you thought through a strategy that will help you achieve it? Does that strategy take into account the value you bring to the company, the perceptions of other workers, the company's policies and culture, and the technical questions that must be answered?

- Do your plans "make sense" in terms of your life? For example, if your at-home game plan requires you and possibly others to work from your home where you are caring for young children, how will you make this work? Or can it work?

- Will the work you plan to do at home yield the money you need to make?

- Do you have the support of those closest to you? For example, if your husband will now have to take over the cooking and cleaning that you've done in the past, is he on board with this? If the change means new or more duties for a colleague back at the office, have you discussed this with him or her?

- And perhaps most important of all, are you being realistic? If your goal is to find a person or company that will hand you eight hours of simple, straightforward work in return for eight hours of pay, you're going to be disappointed. Nothing worthwhile is that simple.

Honestly answering these questions can help you assess the end result you've set out for yourself. Based on your answers, you may have to alter your expectations. Don't be afraid to do this: It's a natural part of the reinvention process. And it's certainly wiser to adjust your vision now than after you've invested a great deal of time, money, and energy.

Prepare for Success

A positive attitude is an asset you can't afford to be without as you make plans for working at home. Sure, you'll probably have some doubts and that's absolutely expected. Work through them with a few trusted people; to the rest of the world you want to appear confident, prepared, and certain of success. Let everything you say and do—from an initial e-mail that announces your intent to build your own website to those playground or cocktail party conversations—convey that attitude. The more you hear yourself describe your plans in clear, positive language, the more you and everyone else will begin to envision this new you.

An important aspect of preparing for success is anticipating disappointment. Wait a minute: We just said you should be positive and forward-looking! We did, but that doesn't mean you close your eyes to the possibility that problems will arise. They will, believe us. But a firm belief in success means you're smart and nimble, not paralyzed by obstacles but able to creatively overcome them.

You'll also want to establish benchmarks for assessing your success. Otherwise, it's hard to know if you've achieved what you set out to. Benchmarks can take all kinds of forms depending on your situation. Here are just a few possibilities:

- Net dollars earned.

- Dollars and hours saved in commuting, work clothes, and lunches out.

- Career advancement.

- Stress reduction for you and your family.

- Progress toward a dream such as owning your own business.

Some of these, like net dollars earned, are easier to gauge than stress reduction or progress toward a dream. But everything can be quantified to some degree, it just takes creativity. Once you decide how you will measure progress, do it regularly, for example every quarter or twice a year. Keep these records as carefully as you would your tax or other financial data. And use it to make midstream corrections.

Two in Your Corner!

As you move forward, we want you to know that we are firmly in your corner. We've been where you're going and we know the satisfaction and success that can come from a closer integration of work and home. It's not simple to get there and it's no slam dunk once you *are* there. But with a thoughtful plan, strong support, the right motivations, and technology on your side, there's nothing stopping you.

Whether your plan is to earn a few extra bucks for incidentals or to build a home-based business with serious growth potential, the time is right to do it from home. Good luck and go for it!

Are You Happy at Home?

Share your successes and keep us posted on your progress by visiting us at womenforhire.com and sending us an email with your comments. We look forward to hearing from you.

appendix

■ ■ ■

Resources for Home Workers

Here's a list of links to explore in a range of key categories related to working from home. An updated and expanded list is available at WomenForHire.com.

Flex-friendly assignments, including some that are home-based, part-time, or contract, can be found by working with these agencies and sites:

- Tentiltwo.com
- Flexjobs.com
- Aquent.com
- On-Ramps.com
- Part-timeProfessionals.com
- IvyExec.com
- MomCorps.com
- FlexibleExecutives.com
- RoseRyan.com

Family-friendly employers that allow work-at-home arrangements for some positions may be found among these sources:

- *Fortune* magazine's 100 Best Companies to Work For: Money.CNN.com/magazines/fortune

- *Fortune* magazine's America's Most Admired Companies: Money.CNN.com/magazines/fortune/mostadmired
- *Working Mother* magazine's 100 Best Companies for Working Mothers: WorkingMother.com
- AARP's Best Employers for Workers over 50: AARPMagazine.org
- The *Information Week 500:* InformationWeek.com
- *Forbes* magazine's 200 Best Small Companies: Forbes.com/lists
- *ComputerWorld*'s 100 Best Places to Work in IT: ComputerWorld.com
- *Black Collegian* magazine's Top 100 Diversity Employers: Black-Collegian.com

Advice and the latest statistics and case studies on flexible work options may be found here:

- WomenForHire.com
- ABCNews.go.com/GMA (Take Control of Your Life segments)
- TelCoa.org
- TeleCommuting.com
- FamiliesAndWork.org
- TeleWorkExchange.com
- EscapeFromCubicleNation .com

National job boards often include postings for work-at-home opportunities, as well as ideas for starting and promoting a home-based service business:

- HotJobs.com
- CareerBuilder.com
- Monster.com
- SimplyHired.com
- Indeed.com
- Sologig.com

- Guru.com
- Elance.com
- Backpage.com
- CraigsList.com
- Idealist.org
- Jobs.com
- MediaBistro.com
- Odesk.com

Sample resources for medical transcription, coding, and billing include:

- MedQuist.com
- PrecyseSolutions.com

Telephone-based customer service agents:

- Telereach.com
- Intrep.com

Online tutoring services:

- Tutor.com
- TutorVista.com
- ASAPTutor.com
- Kaplan.com
- eSylvan.com
- GrowingStars.com
- SmarThinking.com
- National Tutoring Association (NTATutor.org)
- BrainFuse.com

Virtual assistant and concierge services:

- AssistU.com
- VANetworking.com
- TeamDoubleClick.com
- GetFriday.com
- VIPDesk.com
- CharmCityConcierge.com

Home-based virtual customer service agents:

- AlpineAccess.com
- LiveOps.com
- Arise.com
- West.com
- WorkingSolutions.com
- ConvergysWorkAtHome.com

Eldercare agents:

- APlaceForMom.com
- Care.com

Resources for writers:

- Author101.com
- AbsoluteWrite.com
- WritersMarket.com
- Helium.com
- WellFedWriter.com
- MyEssays.com
- FundsForWriters.com
- WriterFind.com
- MediaBistro.com
- ReviewMe.com
- FreelanceWritingGigs.com
- PayPerPost.com
- WorldWideFreelance.com
- BloggingAds.com

Resources to promote your pet-sitting and house-sitting services:

- SitterCity.com
- Care.com
- PetSit.com
- CraigsList.com

Resources for aspiring fitness instructors:

- ACEFitness.org
- National Council on Strength and Fitness (NCSF.org)
- National Strength and Conditioning Association (NSCA-lift.org)

Translation services utilizing home-based workers:

- WeLocalize.com
- The American Translators Association (ATANet.org)
- Telelanguage.com
- SDL.com
- AccuRapid.com

Crafting services:

- ScrapBook.com
- CashCrafters.com
- eBay.com
- Etsy.com

Setting up a website and making money through online advertising:

- 1and1.com
- Blogger.com
- Pages.Google.com
- GoDaddy.com
- Google.com/AdSense

- AdSense.Blogspot.com/
- Publisher.Yahoo.com
- Adbrite.com
- Text-Link-Ads.com

Direct sales companies to explore:

- Direct Selling Association (DSA.org)
- Direct Selling Women's Alliance (DSWA.org)
- AngelaMoore.com
- Arbonne.com
- Avon.com
- BareFootParties.com
- BeadRetreat.com
- BeautiControl.com
- CarlisleCollection.com
- CookieLee.com
- CreativeMemories.com
- DiscoveryToysInc.com
- EssentialBodyWear.com
- EthnicExpressions.com
- FifthavenueCollection.com
- GemStyle.com
- GoldCanyon.com
- HomeandGardenParty.com
- JordanEssentials.com

- LiaSophia.com
- MaryKay.com
- Longaberger.com
- MyPrivateQuarters.com
- OurOwnImage.com
- PartyLite.com
- PrincessHouse.com
- QuietPlacesForYou.com
- Senegence.com
- SignatureHomeStyles.com
- Silpada.com
- Shaklee.com
- ShurePets.com
- SouthernLivingAtHome.com
- StampinUp.com
- TastefullySimple.com
- TheHappyGardener.info
- PamperedChef.com
- TheTravelingVineyard.com
- Tupperware.com
- WorthNY.com

Opportunities for pocket change and little extras:

- ChefsLine.com
- PersonalChefsNetwork.com
- MysteryShop.org
- OnlineVerdict.com
- ZapJury.com
- TrialPractice.com
- DrivingPromotions.com
- AutoWrapped.com

Live guides for search engines:

- Chacha.com
- Mahalo.com

Sources for creative talent and marketing experts to explore:

- OpenAd.net
- Aquent.com
- oDesk.com
- Elance.com

Check these resources before committing to any online or work-at-home opportunity:

- Better Business Bureau (BBB.org)
- Federal Trade Commission (FTC.gov)

Organizational expertise:

- National Association for Professional Organizers (NAPO.net)
- JulieMorgenstern.com
- OrderfromChaos.com

These companies offer tech support for your home-based business and they hire tech experts to work from home to provide remote support:

- GeeksOnTime.com
- GeekSquad.com
- ComputerAssistant.com
- PlumChoice.com
- SupportFreaks.com
- Support.com

These resources offer various aspects of advice when starting a home-based business:

- WhoIs.com
- Open Source Web Design: OSWD.org
- Register.com
- Service Corps of Retired Executives: SCORE.org
- PayPal.com
- The Consolidated Omnibus Budget Reconciliation Act: COBRA.com
- FreelancersUnion.org
- Home Depot Business Tool-Box: HDBusinessToolBox.com
- Small Business Administration: SBA.gov
- Internal Revenue Service: IRS.gov
- National Society of Accountants: NSACCT.org
- Legal information: Nolo.com
- Insurance: Insure.com
- eHealth Insurance Services, Inc.: eHealthInsurance.com
- Business Advice: AllBusiness.com
- National Association for Self-Employed: NASE.org
- National Federation of Independent Business: NFIB.org
- SpringWise.com
- Entrepreneur.com
- StartupNation.com
- Inc. Magazine: Inc.com
- Wall Street Journal Start-up Journal: StartUpJournal.com
- CountMeIn.org
- MyOwnBusiness.com
- BPlans.com
- Business.gov
- MyCorporation.com
- United States Patent and Trademark Office: USPTO.gov

Index